# You Are Somebody Special

## BY

Bill Cosby

Rick Little

Jim Fadiman

Myrtle T. Collins

Charlie W. Shedd

Irene Kassorla

Jim Dobson

Carl Hall

Richard Bolles

Eugene Nida

Edited by Charlie W. Shedd

*For Mike Brice!*

*in friendship*

*Myrtle T. Collins*

*2 April 1979*

McGRAW - HILL BOOK COMPANY

New York    St. Louis    San Francisco

Düsseldorf    London    Mexico    Sydney    Toronto

1 2 3 4 5 6 7 8 9 0 BP  BP 7 8 3 2 1 0 9 8

**Library of Congress Cataloging in Publication Data**

Main entry under title:
You are somebody special.
SUMMARY: Each chapter by a different author
discusses topics of interest to teenagers including,
sex, parents, home life, college, jobs, financial
matters, and religion.
1.   Youth—Conduct of life—Addresses, essays,
lectures.     [1.   Conduct of life]     I.   Cosby, William H.
II.   Shedd, Charlie W.
BJ1661.Y68      170'.202'23      78-8506
ISBN 0-07-056509-0

The authors are grateful to the following for permission to quote passages
from copyrighted material:

Random House, Inc., and Chatto & Windus, Ltd. for *The Past Recaptured*
by Marcel Proust, translated by Andreas Mayor. Copyright © by Chatto
& Windus, Ltd.
W. W. Norton & Co., Inc., for *Conceptions of Modern Psychiatry* by
Harry Stack Sullivan.
Charles E. Merrill Publishing Company for adaptation from *Marriage Has
Many Faces* by Jerome D. Folkman & Nancy Clatworthy, 1970.
A. S. Barnes & Co. for adaptation from *Partners in Love* by Dr. Eleanor
Hamilton.
Alfred A. Knopf, Inc. for *The Prophet* by Kahlil Gibran. Copyright 1923
by Kahlil Gibran; renewal copyright 1951 by Administrators C.T.A. of
Kahlil Gibran Estate and Mary G. Gibran.

# Special Acknowledgments

Special thanks are given to Dr. Charlie W. Shedd for his hours of creativity, out of which evolved the outline for this book. His talent was also used in serving as supervising editor. Appreciation is extended to Carolyn Greene, Marjorie Dold, and Rocky Stensrud, who served on the editorial board, and to Bruce Lee, Senior Editor, of McGraw-Hill.

A very warm and personal thanks to the many high school students and friends who spent hours reviewing and offering suggestions to improve the original manuscripts, and to the eight teachers in Bloomfield Hills, Michigan, and Leipsic, Toledo, and Worthington, Ohio, who piloted this material and offered their constant support and encouragement in the process of its completion. Acknowledgment should also be given to Laurie Stratton for her important contribution in working long hours typing the manuscripts.

Finally, special thanks are expressed to the W. K. Kellogg Foundation, the George Gund Foundation, and the *Reader's Digest* whose financial support has made this project and book possible.

# Contents

vii

# Foreword

A letter to high school students and others who know about life, joy, and struggle:

> We hope this book will speak to you, as possibly few books have before ... because it is about you and all of us, and the concerns we have.
>
> The quest is in your hands now because of a long journey which we have made along with many others. Our journey has taken us through joy, pain, hope, despair, laughter, and tears. These thoughts were born out of our struggles. It is what we wish we had done, but didn't, when we were younger.
>
> Our deepest hope is that through this book (and the course which can go with it) you might avoid some of the struggle and pain we all go through and come to find more joy and fulfillment.
>
> The pages to follow can help you to direct your life through many obstacles and concerns you may face, such as liking yourself more, handling your emotions, being a better friend, getting along with parents, how to be a good parent yourself, and making decisions about money, work, marriage, and the meaning of your life.
>
> So, we leave this book in your hands ... hoping it will serve as a guide from us and others who have traveled some of the paths you may be traveling. We send you our caring and our deepest wishes that your life may be all it can be.
>
> With love,
> Ken Greene
> Rick Little

# William H. Cosby, Jr., Ed.D.

Bill Cosby, whose hilarious stories have touched millions of people for years, revealed his unique gift for laughter at an early age.

In the simplest manner possible, he has become the spokesman of many people all over America. Coming from the Philadelphia ghetto, he represents the voice of the vast ordinary, mediocre world out there. Everyone can seem to identify with some part of his philosophy.

Bill Cosby broke the black barrier on television by winning three Emmy awards for his role in the *I Spy* series. This historic casting of a black man as an equal partner with a white man created international interest in the show and in Bill Cosby.

In 1976 Cosby was awarded his doctoral degree in education at the University of Massachusetts, where he is an adjunct professor of education.

His talent and cool capability have earned him the respect of fellow performers and a vast audience of Cosby fans. This chapter is written by Bill Cosby with the hope that you, too, can earn the respect of others by first understanding "You Are Somebody Special."

# *You Are Somebody Special*

## Sporty

During the years 1951 to 1954 I was in junior high school in Philadelphia. Grades seven through nine. I was not really interested in junior high school in any other activity than watching this fellow named Sporty. That was his nickname.

One day after school I saw Sporty high-jumping. There was no one in the gym with him. He had both high-jump stands up, three old gray cotton-padded mats to break his fall, and a bamboo pole. The bamboo pole was stretched across the standards. (Our pole vaulters used bamboo poles too, so now you know how old I am.)

I watched Sporty jump. He was jumping at 4′ 6″. Now, at that time I was only about 5′ 3″, and very wiry. I watched him jump, and it was interesting. I wanted to do it.

The 4′ 6″ bar looked simple. I watched Sporty make his approach, jump over the bar, and land on the mat. He had on his gym clothes and a very classy-looking pair of rubber-sole track shoes.

Now, the way Sporty jumped and the way I jumped were two different styles. Let's say my style was a sort of running-away-from-the-scene-of-the-crime jump. Sporty's was the classic Eastern Roll.

Sporty approached his target with a certain number of steps, planted his right foot (because he was left-footed), and threw the left leg up. Then as he began to clear the bar, he flattened his body out and kicked his back leg up to keep from knocking the bar off. He also landed smoothly on his back.

So now I tried my style. Coming from his side of the bar, I ran up, stopped, planted both legs and jumped straight up. Then, bringing my knees to my chin, I came down with my behind crashing the bamboo pole. One broken pole!

This, of course, made Sporty very upset. He told me how he had been working in the gym for three weeks by himself; how he had enjoyed high-jumping; how I was the first fool to come in and break his pole. So I apologized and asked him if he would show me how to do it right.

## *Mister Lister*

At that particular point, Mr. Richard Lister came over. Mr. Lister was our gym teacher, a very kind gentleman, who had high-jumped for Temple University. I think his record was 6' 9". Of course to Sporty and me that was out of this world. So when he offered to teach us, we couldn't wait.

I notified my mother I would be home late because Sporty and I were high-jumping. My mother wanted to know if there was a high-jump team. I said, "No, but Sporty and I have a great time just jumping over this bamboo pole." Then she asked me if I had done my homework.

I showed up after school, changed my clothes, came out, and saw Sporty in a gray sweatsuit. First thing: Warm up! Mr. Lister gave us this set of exercises, showing us how we must bend over and do the same things we had done in gym class earlier that day. I notified Mr. Lister that I had done these exercises. Mr. Lister said, "You're going to have to do them again. You have to warm up properly. Get the blood flowing. Loosen up." This, he said, was warning the body it was about to become involved in something special.

So Sporty and I ran around the gym and I thought it was rather silly. Weren't we only making ourselves too tired for jumping over the bar? Needless to say, I found out this was not true, because somehow we had enough energy to jump for the next three hours.

**Jennifer took superior rating in violin at the state music contest this year. There were only three superior ratings in the entire state. This summer at the annual Fourth of July picnic, when all the relatives were there, they asked Jennifer to**

play her prize-winning piece. That afternoon her cousin Beth, thirteen, said, "If only I could play the violin the way you play it!" "Oh, you can," Jennifer answered. (She's always had a sly sense of humor.) "All you need to do is practice two hours a day for seven years. And sometimes you can even have Sundays off."

The author of a best-selling book for teenagers says, "Sure it's sold like crazy. But I had the feeling it would. After all, the manuscript went through twenty-seven drafts before it was finally published."

What's the best thing you do? Could you really be great at it if you would give it more time? Practice it more?

Mr. Lister decided to work on my style, because I had broken three poles already. I had a lot of energy and a lot of drive. This was something I wanted to do, and I enjoyed doing it.

But, of course, I wasn't smooth like Sporty. Sporty had a five-step approach. He marked out his steps, looked at the bar, then started with his right foot. On his fifth step he jumped, threw his left leg up and both arms over, flattened his body out, and landed smoothly on his back. He cleared the bar by six inches. Smooth.

My approach was something else. I stood there, started with my right foot, planted the left down cautiously, and stopped. Then I zigzagged as though I were going to fake the bar out and started up again with three fast steps. As I approached the bar, I made two more adjustment steps, jumped straight up, and brought both legs up in a sitting position. Then I came straight down on top of the bamboo pole, which snapped in half when the pole and I arrived on the mat at the same time.

Needless to say, Sporty was *not* very upset at the fact that if this continued, I might have to go to the hospital for the removal of three bamboo poles.

I also decided maybe this wasn't the sport for me. Somehow when I watched Sporty do it, I thought I could be a jumper. Certainly I had proved that to myself in basketball, when I managed to get more rebounds than most of the other fellows. Certainly I knew I had the coordination, because I was one of the top gym-class athletes. What was the problem?

## Lesson One

Mr. Lister said, "Son, the thing you are going to have to learn is that in order to do anything well, you must start from lesson one. Then we go to lessons two, three, four, and five. These lessons have been written out for you by people who tried them and found they worked. After you have learned these, then it may come to you that this is not necessarily the right way for you. You may then, perhaps, make some adjustments. But, in the meantime, you are fighting yourself."

So Mr. Lister and I worked on a very smooth approach to the bar at the very embarrassing height of two feet. I made my five-step approach, stopped, lifted my left leg, threw my arms up, cleared the bar, and fell on my back.

Mr. Lister said, "Good." And I said, "Yes, but look! A two-foot bar!" He said, "It is better for you to miss at two feet than to break another bar at four feet two. Look how many bars we've saved. You jumped twenty times. You saved twenty bars."

As the months passed, Sporty and I were now jumping at 4' 6". Then Sporty moved the bar to 4' 9". This was indeed a challenge. The bar looked high. At 5' 3", you may be looking eye-to-eye with a 4' 9" bar. I made the approach, and as I approached I became frightened. Not that I would hurt myself, not that I would break the bar—I became frightened because this looked like something I couldn't do.

The closer I got to the bar, the more I realized I couldn't do it. The more I accepted the fact I couldn't, the more I didn't prepare myself physically. In other words, as my mind said no, it allowed certain things to happen so my body would not give its all.

And I did exactly what I thought. I knocked the bar off.

As a matter of fact, the first time I tried it, I remember running up, planting my foot, starting to do it, and then snatching the bar off with my left hand. I never left the ground.

I then put the bar back up. Sporty ran at it, jumped, and his trail leg nicked the bar. But it stayed up. He made 4' 9". Of course, Sporty and I now were competing against each other, and I figured, "If Sporty can do it, I better do it."

I stood on my mark, started with the right foot, and took three steps. Then came that thought again: "Awfully high. You can't make it." Again as I finished the last two steps, I grabbed the bar with my left hand and put it back up. Now Sporty approached the bar again, made his jump, but knocked the bar over. I felt better.

After talking to myself, I decided I could do it now. Suddenly I realized that in being afraid to fail I was making a half-hearted attempt.

So I stood at the mark, tried to block all negative thoughts, and remembered everything positive about myself.

## Six Inches Over

I approached the bar, and for some reason none of the negative thoughts came into play. I jumped, and I found myself looking down on the bar, at least six inches over it. I had cleared that bar, and I was happy.

(What I am doing now is freezing this moment so you can get the actual feeling of what happened: I approached the bar, I planted that foot, jumped with all my might, went up, and went over. I am six inches over, and I say to myself, "I'm up. I'm over. I've done it." Hear the great burst of applause, the cheers from all those little people in my brain. "Yea! We've done it!")

However, I had forgotten to complete the jump, so as I sailed across the bar my trail leg hit. I had actually made the height. Even though I knocked the bar off, I *had* cleared it by a good six inches!

I put the bar up quickly, came back around, and Sporty said, "You know, you really made that." We were both excited, both talking fast, and Sporty, for some reason, felt very good about what I had done.

Again I make my approach with no negative thoughts. Up. Over. Six inches over. This time I remembered to kick and clear that leg.

So 4′ 9″ was no longer a problem. I felt secure. Now I began to think about the next height. If I could do 4′ 9″, looking down on it, how high could I go? 5′ 2″? Impossible! I'm 5′ 3″. How can I jump my height? Wouldn't it be wonderful if I could?

That particular day was a great day for me because I had learned something about myself. I had learned to talk to myself, reason with myself, believe in myself. As long as I could have thoughts stronger than the negatives, I could achieve.

## Football

I went on to Central High in Philadelphia, went out for football, and made the junior varsity. I knew nothing about organized football, but I did make the team, because I was the fastest person there. I know I was the fastest because we had a sprint and I won it.

On the bulletin board, they said you should weigh 135 pounds. I weighed 125.

The junior varsity coach seemed to know many of the players already. He put me on the fifteenth team. This was the first time I ever had on a real football uniform, and I'm not lying when I say I didn't know the plays were already drawn up. I thought plays were called in the huddle and the guys were told where to go. Not by numbers, not by practice, but by saying "I want you to run over there."

So I didn't feel secure, but I was happy to have on the helmet. I was happy to have on the whole uniform. I felt like a real football player, but I was really frightened—fifteenth team! Nothing but skinny linemen, skinny backs. We were the team everybody was supposed to run over.

I'll never forget the day. After the team learned three or four plays, the coach decided there would be a scrimmage. We were on the back lawn near the armory. I was the left halfback. On play 44, the quarterback did a reverse pivot and handed the ball to me. I ran between guard and tackle.

I ran that play with my eyes closed, because I was afraid and I remember feeling as though walls had fallen on me. I remember also a great deal of pain in my front teeth. I had fallen, and my face had hit on the heel of somebody's foot. I remember thinking, "Oh no, my teeth have been knocked out." At that moment, as I reached up and touched my two front teeth (I was very, very proud of them), I questioned if I really wanted to play this game.

Walking back to the huddle and wondering why I was playing, I thought, "Certainly this is a different game than I played on the street." It was a lot more fun there. On the street, I was able to jig and dance and juke the other players. I was one of the best in my neighborhood, and we had some great athletes coming out of our project.

Next play they called 22, which was the right halfback running between guard and tackle. All I do now is fake like I'm getting a pitchout, and the right halfback gets creamed. This didn't make sense. I thought, "I'll finish the practice, turn in my uniform, and do something else. Run cross country. Go out for debate."

## Touchdown

The next play was 44 again. I thought, "This time they are not going to hit my face." (In those days there were no face guards.) As the quarterback handed me the ball, I kept my eyes open and for some weird reason there was a space to run through. I hit that space fast because I didn't want anyone to touch me.

They didn't. Since there were no goalposts I thought, "I'll run as far as I can go so it will have to be a touchdown." We could have been on the one-yard line. After ninety-nine yards or something like that, I heard the coach's whistle. He whistled six or seven times, and I remember him screaming, "Someone catch him before he runs into the locker room."

I came running back with the ball tucked under my arm, and I had the greatest feeling. I had scored a touchdown. There was a big smile on my face, which I quickly took off before I got back to the coach. You have to act cool, you know, after you've done something great.

Then, of course, the thing that always happens after success is—can you do it again? I didn't know.

The next play we ran was 22 again, and once more the

poor kid got smeared. Then another 44 and I got smeared. I wondered once more if it was too late for cross country. But I had already scored once, so I had a feeling that I could do it again and again and again.

When we finished practice, walking back up that hill, I knew the other players were looking at me because I had done something nobody else had done that day. I scored a touchdown. Even the guys on the first team hadn't scored.

Next day I came back to practice, warmed up, and I was a different person mentally. I was somebody special. I felt they were all looking at me—they all knew who I was.

Sure enough, we got into another scrimmage, because we were preparing for our first game against Gratz High School. We ran the old 44, and I broke loose and ran for another touchdown. Well, now I knew I was good. When I came back, the fellows on the fifteenth were all clapping for me. Still, I didn't let the coach see me smile, but inside I was as happy as I could be.

The next day the coach said, "Cosby, you're now on the second team. Second team, left halfback." I smiled. That day in scrimmage, I ran another touchdown—same old 44.

### First Team

To make a long story short, I became the first-string left halfback. Now my reputation reached the varsity. Some kid down there on the JVs was running touchdowns left and right!

As I was getting dressed with my little 125-pound self, I tried to swell up like 135. I noticed some of the varsity players who had showered with me were looking at me. So I puffed myself up to look real strong, muscular. I felt good about that.

Self-confidence has a lot to do with your performance—

how well you perform, how much success you have, and even if you do not succeed, how much progress you are making.

One or two questions here. You might ask, "Where is my uniqueness?" The answer to that is—*in your mind!*

> "Do you know how I feel right now? It is as though I am really not a person at all. What I am is a robot. All my life my mom has been telling me what to do and expecting me to do it. In high school it is the teachers. Now my boyfriend says if only I would listen to him, everything would be great. Well, sometime I hope I get around to being Sally."
> —*From a high school student's thoughts about herself.*

When you begin to choose something you like to do, something you want to do, you can also enter areas you have never tried before. You can become successful, but first you must have some sort of feeling for it. How do you get a feeling about it? Sometimes the answer is "try." If you don't try, you will never know.

> What is success?
>
> What have you accepted about yourself?
>
> Who is it you want to be? If you cannot be that person, then who will you be?

The choices are up to you. The possibilities are wide open.

An ancient philosopher asked,
"What art thou, oh man, but a
wretched creature appointed to
carry a carcass up and down?"

The Psalmist wrote, "I am fearfully
and wonderfully made."

We all have times when we feel
like the philosopher, and days when
we think the Psalmist must be right.
But most of the time, which way
do you feel?

# RICK LITTLE

Rick Little is a young man whose sensitivity, openness, and ability have brought him success at an early age. He is a popular speaker for high school and college assemblies, a counselor and youth leader. His awareness of the struggles involved in being a high school and college student has led him to become the founder and president of Quest, Inc. Quest has organized a national coalition of experts who are addressing the real-life personal concerns of teenagers throughout the United States.

# *You and Your Feelings*

Sandy is a high school senior. She's in the band and on the girls' track team. She graduates this year and is planning to study nursing at a state university.

Sandy is one of ten high school juniors and seniors who helped write this chapter. They described what it's like to feel lonely, depressed, inferior, afraid, embarrassed, jealous, happy, confident, free, and loved.

## Out of It

Here's part of a letter from Sandy to one of her friends:

Do you know what really bothers me? This may sound weird, but it's that I haven't cried for a long time. I never did cry much, but I wish I could, because I'm really hurting inside.

Maybe what's bothering me most is that nobody knows how I feel. But I guess I shouldn't expect anyone to, because I never say anything about it.

Lately I've been doing a lot of thinking when I can find the time to be alone and away from everybody. I have been thinking about my life and my friends and have just about decided that I'm a loner. But I don't really want to be. I just want to be happy for a change.

> Do you ever feel like Sandy?
>
> When you feel that way, do you withdraw from people?
>
> Have you figured out why you don't talk to someone?
>
> When did you decide you couldn't talk to anyone?

Sandy is like many people: struggling through school, sometimes feeling lonely and left out.

And it doesn't make much difference whether you're popular, on the football team, in the band, or in the French Club. You're likely to experience many times when you feel unwanted, unliked, lonely, and left out.

> Before you read farther, STOP! What is your loneliness factor? Rate yourself from 0 to 10 (zero meaning "very lonely," ten meaning "not lonely").

Tom said he gets those lonely feelings sometimes when he is walking down the halls at school. "It seems like everyone else is talking to someone or having fun, and I'm just an 'extra' . . . like I'm always at the wrong place at the wrong time."

> We were walking down the hall today, just you and me. Then that person came up to you and you talked with him; and talked with him; and talked with him; and all that time I was silent.
>
> *Julie*

**Do you ever feel like this? Left out? Wish you weren't there?**

**Do you have trouble feeling a part of conversations?**

A good friend of mine graduated from high school last year. When we were talking recently he told me that he feels awkward at parties. He doesn't know what to say. He said sometimes he feels maybe he shouldn't go to parties in the first place. Then he wouldn't feel so awkward.

"Looks like everyone else is having a good time. I never feel like I do. Maybe I'm just not as good as they are." Those were his words.

Feeling lonely and "out of it" can be partially overcome if you do two things:

1. Realize that you're not alone. Most of your friends feel lonely as often as you do. And no matter what you do, there will still be times in the future when you feel awkward and "out of it."

2. Take action! Probably the hardest thing when you feel left out is to "push" yourself into the conversation. Jill says, "When I feel left out, it helps to remember that

a lot of the other kids are probably in the same position. So in trying to help them feel more comfortable, the conversation gets easier for both of us."

## *I Give Up*

Jeff is seventeen. Life hasn't been easy for him. His father is an alcoholic, and Jeff has had a difficult time trying to accept and understand the situation.

Jeff's problem began three years ago when his mother was killed in a car accident. His father, who had already been drinking too much, began drinking even more. This worried Jeff, and more than that, it seemed he was losing his dad, too.

During his sophomore year, Jeff's grades really dropped. Then he quit his part-time job. He quit basketball, dropped out of track, and became almost impossible to talk to. His friends felt sorry for him, but no one knew how to help him.

Late in his junior year, Jeff's girlfriend, Susan, broke off their relationship. "I can't watch you destroy yourself, your friends, me, and everyone else along with you," she said. "I know you've had it tough, Jeff. I'm really sorry about that. But just because you are willing to live in those feelings of sorrow the rest of your life doesn't mean I'm willing to go along with you."

Frank words. Bold and piercing. What Susan said shook Jeff hard, and he missed school for several days. Most of the time he sat alone in his room.

What would you do if all this happened to you?

What could Jeff have done to handle his feelings better?

If you were one of Jeff's friends, can you think of some specific things

**you could have said (something you could have done) to help Jeff with his feelings?**

Jeff's father tried to help. He made several attempts, but Jeff wouldn't talk. After three days, Susan came to see him. "Jeff," she began, "I'm really sorry I hurt you by what I said. I just wanted you to see what's happening to you. Where you're headed."

Jeff raised his eyes and looked at her, then turned away. Susan moved near the window where Jeff was sitting and sat next to him.

"See those few flowers in the garden?" she asked. Jeff glanced out the window for a quick moment as though he wasn't too interested.

"You and I planted those flowers a few weeks ago, Jeff. Do you remember?" Jeff, uncaringly, shrugged his shoulders and muttered to himself, "So?"

"Look at them, Jeff. Those flowers have been through rain, wind, frost, and your dog has even trampled through the garden. And still they're alive and growing. Just like you in a lot of ways. Nothing has been easy for you. But you're still here. You're breathing! You're alive! If you separate yourself from hardships, your life doesn't have much meaning. Happiness comes through working out problems and overcoming difficulties. Even babies come through the pain and suffering of a mother. That's how it is. That's how it can be with you. You can rise above your problems."

As Jeff lifted his head, Susan noticed a tear. It ran down his cheek and he brushed it away. For a long time no one talked.

Then Jeff placed his hand on Susan's and said, "It's kind of funny, this whole thing. Until now, I never thought about how you put it. Like that flower. I can see what you mean. I guess I have been unfair to myself and everyone. Especially you."

When things get tough for you, it's important to remember that your life is part of something bigger than you. You are a part of something "before" you and something "after" you. The problem in your life, no matter what it is, no matter how big it may seem, is little more than a fleeting moment on the time line of eternity. And if you give yourself the chance, your problem can become a source of your own future happiness.

> Snow and storm
> And a road full of stones,
> Strengthens the muscles
> And hardens the bones.
> *—Old Scandinavian*
> *proverb*

## Everyone Is Better

I always lose, you always win. I always fail, you always pass. I'm always late, you're always on time. I'm always left out, you're always included. I'm always sitting around, you're always busy.

Well, I have been thinking about this a lot and there just has to be something I can do better than you. If only I could find what it is. You know I think you are neat, but I don't really want to be a carbon copy of you. I want to be me.

*Julie*

It's hard when we feel as if our friends are always better at things than we are.

Julie is starting on the right road when she says, "There must be something I can do better than you."

> Do you sometimes try too much to be like someone else? Make a list of the ways you feel (even a little bit) you've been trying to duplicate someone else. Then make an honest list of things that are unique about you which others may be copying.

At the bottom of her note, Julie wrote:

I think when I find myself, I will also find a reason for living, a reason for dying, and a reason for everything else.

> So how do we find ourselves?
> How do we think more positively about ourselves?

You can begin by realizing that getting to know yourself is a lifelong process. And don't get too discouraged if it seems that you aren't getting anywhere. Only by opening yourself up and becoming vulnerable will you begin to learn more about the "real you." You may be even a little surprised at the kind of person you find. Not quite what you expected.

## Spooks in the Attic

KIM: When I feel afraid, my first reaction is to hide my feelings. When I get scared, I try to pretend everything is okay. I get this funny feeling inside, hoping no one will notice. Then I start acting differently.

RON: The hardest thing for me when I'm afraid is to admit it. I feel like I shouldn't be afraid. So, instead of facing it, I try to bury it and act like it isn't there. Sometimes it works, but most of the time it just makes things worse.

Like Kim and Ron, most of us find it difficult to share our feelings openly. We bury them, try to forget them, deny them, or pretend they don't exist. It's even possible to bury feelings so deeply we don't know they exist.

Sometimes the reason we bury feelings is to protect ourselves from unhappy memories . . . like the death of a friend, the loss of a parent, or an argument between parents when somebody got hurt . . . maybe you.

Other times, like Kim and Ron we hide our feelings for a short while when we are afraid or angry. This kind of buried feeling normally doesn't last long. It's like painting an old car to make it appear more attractive when you want to sell it. You know it doesn't change the rust or the age. But it does cover the problem temporarily.

### Embarrassed

Bob was a super athlete. In grade school he played on the midget football team. During junior high he was first-team fullback. Then came high school and things were different. Here's the story Bob told us.

"All my life I wanted to play football. When I was little, my dad and I used the living room for a field and we played every night when he came home from work. We used a little sponge as the ball and had to be really careful of the lamps and furniture. My mom never did like the idea.

"At supper, I remember my dad always said, 'Bob, you've got to eat up so you get big and strong like daddy.' To me, he was a real giant. I was pretty small for my age, but he always told me if I kept eating I'd be as big as him someday. So, I kept eating.

"When I was eleven, I joined the midget football team. It was great! We practiced every day for two hours. The rest of the day I ran through the house (football in hand) yelling 'Green... 42, ready... hut, hut, hut. Mom arranged for a babysitter.

"Then came junior high. Each year I made first-team fullback for my grade. I loved it and my dad came to all the games. I was still pretty small. In fact, the smallest on the team.

"When I reached high school, everything changed. The first time I went to the locker room my sophomore year to get fitted for my uniform, six seniors stole my jeans and hung them on a ceiling light. I was too small to get them down and too embarrassed to ask for help.

"Luckily, the coach walked by and helped me out.

"After a few weeks of practice came a scrimmage. When the coach said all the sophomores had to hold dummies for scrimmage, I didn't understand what was about to happen. I learned fast. [In football, a dummy is a large cushioned pad held up to represent a player. The blocker is supposed to hit this pad and "make room" for a runner.]

"A 260-pound senior came charging toward me. I weighed 125. He was grunting and making some really funny faces. I was about to laugh when he lowered his head and came trampling over me. When I opened my eyes and saw several people looking down at me, I realized I had been carried to the locker room, unconscious. The coach kept putting this terrible-smelling stuff under my nose until I finally put my head up and said 'I'm okay.' But I felt totally humiliated."

Have you had times when you've felt really embarrassed? Humiliated? What was your "comeback"? Did you quit or keep on trying?

**What would you do if it happened again?**

Today Bob is a senior. He's first-team fullback for his school and weighs 180.

"At first I felt like quitting. But the more I thought about it, I realized I'd only be hurting myself. And I would be setting a pattern for my future of quitting every time I got embarrassed or hurt."

Perseverance doesn't come easy, that's for sure. But if you realize (as Bob did) that you are setting a life pattern with every decision you make, you may find it easier to develop perseverance.

## Jealousy

Nancy was walking toward her locker when she noticed her boyfriend, Tony, talking with Carol. Nancy and Carol don't get along. They are rivals in almost everything. Especially Tony.

Nancy walked to her locker and tried to pretend she didn't notice Tony and Carol. It didn't work. Carol spotted her, grabbed Tony's arm, and pulled him toward Nancy's locker. She was giggling and Tony was apparently having a good time. He was unaware of the jealousy between the two girls.

As they approached, Nancy tried to act as if it didn't bother her. But inside she was raging with jealousy and resentment.

**Ever happen to you?**
**What did you do?**

Do you get jealous easily? What kinds of things make you jealous?

Rate yourself on a scale of 0 to 10 (zero meaning "I'm a very jealous person," ten meaning "I'm not a jealous person").

Have you become more jealous of friends, boyfriend, or girlfriend in the past year or two? If so, why?

What are the biggest causes of jealousy among teenagers? Our group of juniors and seniors decided on five (in order of frequency):

1. Your boyfriend or girlfriend is spending a lot of time with someone else.

2. When the same people are always selected first for special projects and assignments.

3. If a group of your friends gets together and you don't get asked to go with them.

4. Other people who have better clothes, a nicer car, more spending money, or other material things.

5. Looks. It's hard if you aren't very good-looking not to be jealous of those who are. They seem to be more popular, have more dates, and do more things.

**Do you agree with these?**

**Can you think of more?**

You are not born with jealousy. You do not inherit it. Instead this is something you develop by watching others. We learn to be possessive, to guard and protect what we *think* is ours. We build fences around our area and if someone intrudes, jealousy flares.

Jealousy can be a problem. It's difficult and nearly impossible to overcome fully, but it is possible to control. Left uncontrolled, jealousy can destroy relationships and create a lifetime of misery and insecurity.

Jill and Sandy, who are among the ten who contributed to our discussion, say that for them, jealousy is the biggest problem in their relationships with boyfriends. "Even little things, like talking to someone else during class, make him mad."

Suggestions?

1. Accept your feelings of jealousy as normal. When you're threatened by someone who could take away your "special person," it is normal to be jealous.

2. WARN YOURSELF! Too much jealousy can destroy the very thing you love. You might chase away the person you want most.

3. Tell your girlfriend or boyfriend you feel jealous and threatened. "I really feel bad when I see you talking with——" He or she will probably respond with something like "But they were only asking me the homework assignment for English." Now it's in the open. She's aware of the real feelings. So is he. And hopefully this will open the door for better communications in the future.

## Freedom

Do you know how it feels to be free? Does being free mean "being yourself"? Or is freedom something none of us will ever really experience? What does freedom mean to you? What is it?

There are many barriers to what some think of as freedom. Ron, Kim, Sandy, Jill, and Jeff say their biggest barriers to freedom are parents, school, friends, church.

### PARENTS

"My parents expect too much from me. They have my whole life planned out. Like what I should do when I graduate, when I should get married, even the college I should attend."

"Not mine. My parents couldn't care less where I go, what I do. For me, that's just as bad. Maybe worse."

"My parents' biggest gripe is school. They get upset if I get too many C's. And if I get a D, I might as well not go home. But it's not my fault. The trouble is they won't let me take the subjects I want. And when I ask 'Why?' they say those courses won't help me in 'real life.'"

### SCHOOL

"It isn't fair. I study the things that really interest me and then get tested on what I didn't study. So I get poor grades and get hassled at home for not studying, but I really did. On the wrong things."

"I don't think we're really free at school to pursue our own interests and things we're good at doing. Instead, we memorize and learn whatever we're told is important for us."

"I don't feel free in school because everything is too structured. In the middle of a good discussion, the bell rings. Then I'm supposed to forget that discussion and take a test in some other subject."

### FRIENDS

"Sometimes I feel like I'm not really free to be myself and to say what I'm thinking."

"It seems to me people are like fish . . . they form schools. Everybody thinks the same, acts the same, talks the same, goes the same places, takes the same classes. Nobody feels free to be an individual."

"I feel sort of free with my friends except when we're all together in a group. Then I don't think any of us are very free. Everything we talk about is superficial. It's all on the surface. Nobody feels open enough to talk about real problems and feelings."

### CHURCH

"I always feel like I have to act a certain way when I go to church. Everybody sits straight, keeps quiet, says nice things to each other, and has to stay awake when they're really tired. I don't feel free to wear what I want because I have to dress up. And I sure don't feel free to disagree with my minister."

"Church is so one-sided. It's like they're the only ones with the answers. And if I disagree or take a stand, I'm alone. It's like everyone is afraid to think."

"I really like church. It helps me sort things out. Except one thing: I don't like other people forcing their beliefs on me. They don't always do that, but sometimes I feel like they think I'm not good enough to have my own ideas. And that inhibits me in the group."

Freedom. It's something most of us want, but few of us are ever able to define or pin down what we really mean by freedom. One important thing we realized in our group is that all the barriers to freedom we thought of are surface things. Not very deep.

There are many ways to be free. Graduation and leaving home may be two of them. But it's like Ron says: "We think once we're out of school and leave home, we'll be free. Maybe we will be, but not for long. Wherever we go and whatever we do there will be other barriers."

How would you describe a person
who is "free"?

Are you?

Freedom, as used in this section, is a process of learning
to keep a good feeling about yourself, no matter what situation you are in. Sometimes you can be free if you change
your environment (school, home, friends). But that's only
surface change. To become free inside, there's one important concept you need to know and practice:

*Do not allow yourself to become tied to events.*

Example?

TOM:   When I missed that shot I lost the game! It's all
my fault. We could have won. I'm no good. The team
would be better off without me. I can't do anything right.

This was an example of allowing the event to be in control. Here's an alternative . . . a way to become more free:

Instant replay:

TOM:   I blew it! I shouldn't have missed that shot. I
could have made it. I did have some other good plays,
though. I'm not a bad player. Just because I missed an important shot doesn't make me worthless. I'm still okay.

The biggest difference between these examples is Tom's
attitude about himself. He did miss an important shot.
Maybe he could have won the game for his team. But he
didn't. Now what?

By not allowing yourself to become tied to events, you
can learn to keep a good feeling about yourself, no matter
what situation you are in. By feeling okay about yourself,
you may even find your game improves. You accept the
situation, move beyond it, and make changes as they're
needed.

This process of becoming free will work no matter what situation you're in. It may take years, maybe a lifetime. But it's the kind of thing which grows with patience, practice, and commitment.

An alcoholic parent, mental illness in your family, trouble with friends, poor grades—all of these barriers to freedom can be overcome. You can be free.

Freedom is not yesterday and it is not tomorrow.
Becoming free is a daily job.
Each day we need to free ourselves of yesterday
        and the worries of tomorrow.
So we live these moments.
But we accept this truth:
        Freedom doesn't give us the right to live exactly
            as we want.
        Freedom doesn't mean we are separated from pressure;
            it doesn't mean we have the right
                to hurt other people
        Or get in the way of their freedom.
It does mean we begin to accept ourselves as worthwhile.
Regardless of our age, problems, or situations.


## Confidence

For some people, confidence is something to think about, dream about, or wish for. It's far off in wonderland. Too far to reach.

In Chapter 1, Bill Cosby told how he built confidence in himself. He never thought he could jump as high as 4'6". Then as he practiced and built confidence in his ability, he was able to jump 4'9". Even higher.

Believing in yourself is hard if your past is full of "dropouts," "nice tries," and "maybe next times." Those next times never seem to come. Can't get a date ... flunked history . . . forgot my lines in the play . . . wrecked my parents' car. Each time something like this happens, your self-confidence takes a dive. So next time, you're not quite as enthusiastic. The excitement is gone. You may not even be willing to try. "I goofed once. That's bad enough, right?"

TODD: "Nobody ever listens to me. It's like I'm not important to them."

DOUG: "I don't think I'm very likeable. I don't have fun with other people. Most of the time I'd rather be left alone."

JILL: "I'll never do anything important. I can't really control what happens to me anyway. And even when I try my best, everything turns out wrong."

Sound like someone you know?

Laurie describes the feeling of confidence. And she also tells what could happen to you:

"I always enjoyed art but never tried anything creative. I didn't think it would turn out too well. Then, my junior year, the art teacher asked me to make an eagle. It was a special art project and I was really nervous at first. I kept putting it off, making up silly excuses. Finally, the teacher gave me two more weeks to finish. So, I began to work. Making that eagle was really fun. The more I worked, the more I didn't want to quit. I finished the eagle on time. At the end of the year I received an art award."

Are there times you've tried something and quit?

Are there things you would like to have done but didn't start because you were afraid you might fail?

> Could confidence be the willing-
> ness to take another risk after you
> feel you have failed?
>
> Could confidence be a decision?

Confidence is developed through accepting yourself. Feeling confident is like freedom. It doesn't happen overnight. It builds as you learn to keep trying, even when you don't feel confident. It's important to remember confidence comes from little successes, no matter how little. These little successes can lead to bigger successes and increased confidence in yourself.

## Love

Love is something we all feel. Sometimes it may be called by another name, but it's love. Most of us have never tried to define it. We just knew it was there and that was good enough. But since love is such an important feeling, our group decided to discuss it.

> If love is happiness
>    Why is there sadness?
> If love is kind
>    Why is there pain?
> If love is understanding
>    Why are there fights?
> If love is sharing
>    Why is it possessive?
> If love is for me
>    Why don't I feel it?
> If love is free
>    Why are people cheated?
> If love has no boundaries
>    Why don't we love?

If love is enduring
  Why does it die?
If love is me
  Why don't I love you?
If love is you
  Where are you?
If love is here
  Where am I?
If love has many sides
  Why can't I find one?
If love can reach me
  Here I am!

ENTERPRISE, KANSAS
—*Sandy Karl*

Do you feel loved? Wanted? Does anyone care about you?

SUE:   Sometimes it seems like nobody really loves. Nobody really cares. Everyone is trying too hard to watch out for himself. My parents haven't said "I love you" since I was little.

TOM:   All this talk bothers me. Everybody's sitting here saying there's no love. Nobody cares. Well, I don't agree. My parents love me, and they show it. Every day they show it by the little things they do. Just because people don't throw their arms around you every time you walk in the house doesn't mean there's no love. Real love isn't always something you can see. Maybe you don't even need to see it if you know it's there.

Love means different things to different people. Some think of love as mature caring. Some think of it as sex. Others think of God when they hear the word. And there are all kinds of definitions focusing on such words as patience, kindness, humbleness, generosity, sensitivity, fairness, warmth.

> What is your definition of love?
>
> How does it feel when you are loved?

In the past, girls have been more open to being labeled loving, warm, and tender. Boys have resisted these labels. Somehow, to be a loving, warm, affectionate male means you're weak, fragile, "sissy."

Many of these stereotypes still exist. But others today are beginning to understand that real love requires real strength. Confidence, capability, dependability, all have a strong sound, don't they?

Love has a way of healing, too. To be loved gives life new meaning. Purpose, joy, peace, fulfillment, pride... these all come to us when we know someone loves us. And the more love we give others, the greater we feel ourselves.

> Is my life a shout in an empty forest
>     Or did someone hear and will they remember?
> An echo answered my silent question:
>     Are you chained to yourself? ... go and care.
> Is there not one person left to touch? ... go and love.
>                                    *by Ken Greene*

## How Can I Become More Feeling?

FIRST ... *Be aware of your feelings.*

1. Explore your emotions and seek to discover their meaning. Feelings like love, anger, envy, freedom, hurt, joy, jealousy, sadness, trust, hate, are all only a small part of the

"real you." The feelings you have about yourself, your mother and father, your friends, or God—these don't have to be labeled good or bad. *Feelings are!* They are the essence of you. Through becoming aware of them, you become more fully aware of yourself.

2. Attempt to clearly define your feeling in one word. Bitter, calm, defensive, fearful, proud, lonely, weak, guilty, inferior, confused, embarrassed, angry, jealous, peaceful, loved. This is an excellent practice because it helps you understand and express your feelings more fully.


SECOND . . . *Accept your feelings.*

1. Understand that some of your feelings are only temporary. They won't last forever.

2. To become sensitive to your feelings is like learning to play the piano or throw a football. It takes practice.

3. Say it again—feelings, no matter what they are, don't have to be labeled either good or bad. It's okay to feel lonely, embarrassed, afraid. It's okay to feel lots of things. As long as you keep your feelings in check or in balance with the rest of you.

4. Understand that most of your feelings need no defense. What matters is that the feeling exists: It doesn't have to be explained or justified.

5. Accept the fact that your feelings are personal. Even if other people feel what you feel, yours are unique with you.


THIRD . . . *Express your feelings.*

1. Express your feelings as they are felt. Don't let them build up inside to a danger level which makes you self-destructive.

2. Talk to your close friends about your feelings. Open up. Sure, you may get hurt if you expose yourself, but you

may also realize your own inner power. You might discover new strength. In addition, your openness may inspire someone else to be open.

3. Express your feelings in as nice a way as you can. Remember, feelings expressed in a thoughtless way defeat the purpose of being open. You don't want to build barriers. You want to remove them.

## Creed for Me

I will be kind to myself.
I will take time to enjoy my feelings.
Sometimes I get so wrapped up in
    School,
      Clubs,
        Church,
          Social life,
            Just messing around
I forget to enjoy myself.
Since I have a choice
It makes sense for me to work at feeling
    Positive,
    Happy,
    Free.
This way I will become all I can become.
If I do this
I will enjoy life more.
And I will enjoy being me!

# JIM FADIMAN

James Fadiman, Ph.D., is a lecturer at Stanford University and at the California Institute for Transpersonal Psychology. He has also taught at the University of California in San Francisco.

Dr. Fadiman is on the editorial boards of several journals, has edited *The Proper Study of Man* and co-edited *Exploring Madness, Relax,* and *Transpersonal Education.* He is co-author with Robert Frager of *Personality and Personal Growth.* He has also lectured and led workshops internationally. Most recently he has become involved with the movement for Integral Medicine, and has spoken about it at medical conferences and on national television. In person, as well as from the stage, Dr. Fadiman's humor and sensitivity have a way of reaching into the hearts of his audience, bringing about positive change.

# *You and Your Attitudes*

## What Are Your Limits?

Trying to answer this question is difficult because it implies that you can see the future. Let's start by cutting this down to an answerable size. What can't you do?

"I can't get my homework in on time."
"I can't buy a stereo."
"I can't fit into a size 9 dress."

"I can't get a job."
"I can't get a date."
"I can't make the team."
"I can't please my parents."
"I can't drive a motorcycle."

The list goes on. Each of us has tried to accomplish something or learn something, and failed. If you try and try and don't succeed, it's natural to stop trying. You may want to give up, to accept the failure as evidence that you *can't* succeed and *won't* ever. Once you've found a personal limitation, the safe thing to do is to avoid times and places where you might be asked to try again and turn to something else. That's safe, that's secure—only it doesn't work. It doesn't work because you can't protect yourself from new situations, new friends, new teachers, new problems.

If you decide you're no good at math, the world doesn't stop making numbers. If you're in school, numbers keep coming at you. The same thing is true if you're balancing a checkbook, getting paid for a job, buying clothes, or filling out tax forms. Your limitation doesn't go away. So, there is only one thing to do—change it! (You *can* change it, but since you don't believe me yet, don't worry about it.)

All you need to consider now is that you have some limits. Some of your limits you know about. Others you probably don't know yet. But you also know that you shy away from places where you have failed. So, knowing that you have limitations is the first step in overcoming them.

## Where Did Your Limits Come From?

Strange as it may seem, most of us learned our limits when we were small. We were taught to have limits. Subtle teaching, but real. How could that be? The process goes like this:
When you were born, you were pure potential. No limits.

As an infant, you didn't do much—a little wiggling, a lot of sleeping, some eating, some smiling, some crying. At that time, you might have become anything.

If you've seen a newborn baby, you know this is a fact—you can't tell whether this baby will become a carpetlayer, an executive secretary, a mountain climber, rock singer, nurse, or lathe operator. Sure, if you know whether it's a boy or girl you can tell some things. But the only thing you can really tell about any child's future is that there is still abundant opportunity and potential.

The first few years of life are times of incredible learning. Infants learn to use all the muscles of their body, to balance themselves, to distinguish thousands of colors, to tell hundreds of textures and odors. They learn to pick up the meaning of changes in voice or facial gestures. They learn to speak a language without any idea of what the language is.

In the first four years of life you learned more easily, more quickly, more effectively, and more simply than you ever will again. Children assume that anything and everything is possible. For them, limitation is their size and age, both of which they are planning to overcome.

That's how it was with you. But about the time school began, other things started happening. Along with learning how to talk and to understand people, you also learned to believe what you were told. Do you remember your opinions of Santa Claus, the Easter Bunny, or the Tooth Fairy? Chances are you've changed your ideas by now, but try to recall your total acceptance of what your parents said. For a while, you accepted anything your parents told you as an absolute truth.

You believed your parents for several reasons. One was that they were the most important people in your life. They controlled most of the things you wanted. They also spent more time with you than anyone else. They listened to your needs more than anyone. They were the biggest people in your life.

Sometimes it seemed your parents were giants, physically towering over you. They were like gods. They told you when to get up, when to eat, when to go to the bathroom, what to wear, where to play, when to share, when to sleep. Since you believed them in all those things, it's natural you would believe them about everything else.

As you think about it, you will remember many obvious things you learned from your parents. Many of these you have outgrown. But you also learned from them many things which you may not be aware of, like habits and attitudes. Some may be helpful. Some may not. Do you get angry easily? Are you critical? Are you especially hard on yourself when you make a mistake? Do you lack confidence? If the answer is "Yes" to any of these, ask yourself, "Which one of my parents has those traits?" Remember, though, that some of the finest qualities you have also come from your parents. It is natural to gain both strengths and limitations from our parents. None of us is perfect. Some of the behaviors you learned from your mother and father may have placed limitations on your individual potential.

Here's how it works:

Imagine you are four years old and you are eating your dinner. You reach for your milk but you don't get a firm grip on it.

*Crash!* A pool of milk covers part of the table and begins to cascade to the floor. Your mother or father says, "You are so clumsy! Go get that mess cleaned up!"

You don't know what clumsy means, but you figure out that it has something to do with milk. Later on you spill some orange juice, and once again you hear "You are so clumsy, I don't know what to do with you."

"Aha!" you think. "Clumsy doesn't have to do only with milk. It also has something to do with spilling things." Being a reasonable child, you may look for a chance to spill something else to see if you have it figured out.

Another meal, another spill, your father says to your mother, "Clumsy did it again."

You are embarrassed by your actions but you have learned two things—being "clumsy" has to do with spilling and dropping things, and you, not the glass or the milk, are "clumsy."

Now a strange thing happens. You want to be the kind of person your parents *tell you to be* because you feel that your parents tell the truth about the world, and you must depend on them.

You have been told a few times you are clumsy. You know what it means, you know how to do it, and it is true that you do clumsy things sometimes. (Notice: *sometimes* —not always.) You are like anyone else, but now you can guess what happens.

You grow up. You begin to make your own decisions and have your own opinions. You become more independent. You listen to other people now, but you also decide some things for yourself.

You are no longer completely dependent on your parents' point of view. You have your own experiences to rely on. And you don't even remember that your parents yelled at you for spilling milk, or that they called you clumsy. That was years ago!

Then one day you find yourself in a situation where you feel a little bit tense and you do something "clumsy." "Oh no!," you say to yourself. "I'm so clumsy. I always do the wrong thing."

You have learned that response from your parents.

Now, as you continue to grow up, you begin to inhibit some of your normal capacity to make sure, confident movements. You begin to limit yourself because you're afraid of doing something clumsy.

Then comes a time at school when everyone in your class is starting to play kickball. You start too. The first times you are not so good. In fact, you are clumsy. What you don't notice is that everyone else is clumsy too. But what you feel is another evidence of *your* clumsiness.

You hang back. You don't try very hard. You say, "I don't like this game. It's dumb." After a while, as other kids continue to play, you see that you aren't as good as they are.

You have become truly clumsy because you *know* you won't improve easily.

This vicious circle can extend to more and more activities as you mature. In high school, you'll see it being repeated in every gym class and at dances.

Ever hear this exchange?

A: Do you dance?

B: No, I don't like to.

A: Ever tried?

B: Well, no. But I don't like it.

A: How do you know you don't like it if you never tried it?

B: Well, I just know. It looks silly. Besides, it doesn't look like much fun.

Translation: "I'm too clumsy to dance. I'd like to but I'm afraid to try. It's easier to put it down than to admit that I might fail."

Now here's a crazy thing about all of this—when you do something gracefully, successfully, or even elegantly, you tend to overlook that and only notice the times when you are clumsy.

Many times we do things which could really make us feel good if we only noticed. My older brother, Jeff, played basketball in high school. He was tall, fast, strong. He threw good passes, and he shot well. He was not a star, but he was good. However, he never saw that he was good.

If you asked Jeff how he was playing, he would talk about his over-all awkwardness. He would say, "I have the worst form of anyone on the team." This was Jeff's idea of Jeff. What he had done was overlook any part of his playing which was good. He was totally focused on those parts which reinforced his earlier childhood ideas of being clumsy.

What Jeff had done was set up a limitation. Then he kept himself confined by that limitation, even when he was doing well. He didn't know what it was to feel "coordinated and skilled." He'd never learned that experience.

## The Four-Minute Mile

Once it was an accepted fact that the mile couldn't be run under four minutes. Runners believed it; coaches believed it; fans believed it.

Some people believed it so much they wrote articles that "proved" the theory. The human body was only strong enough, fast enough, to run the mile in four minutes. No less, ever.

Then one day a man named Roger Bannister ran the mile in under four minutes. He defied the experts and did the *seemingly* impossible.. Then it began to happen often. Other runners broke the four-minute mile regularly. Within the first year and a half after Roger Bannister ran the four-minute mile, more than a dozen others broke that magic barrier.

Remember that any limit you feel has held you back in the past doesn't have to confine you in the future. Each of us is much more capable of great accomplishments than we give ourselves credit for. Like the runners who broke the four-minute mile, each of us can push through old boundaries if we want to.


## Exceptional Abilities

In biology there is a saying "If it is true for one member of the species, it's true for the species." Meaning? If you can find one member of the species with a special trait or ability, then that ability is possible for any member of that same species. If one person can run a mile in four minutes, it's fair to say *any* person *might* be able to run a mile in four minutes. Too many of us have limitations that start with "Nobody can...," "It's impossible to...," "No one could ever...."

Let's look at a few well-documented unusual abilities that are true for some human beings and therefore possible for any of us. (Not easy, but *possible*.)

I was raised to think there were two levels of abilities. First there were normal abilities like being able to sing, swim, play the flute, or do calculus. Then there were the exceptional abilities like ESP or a photographic memory. People who did those things were "special," "different," or "strange." Or maybe no one could really do those things. Maybe the reports were fairy stories—nonsense to fool the gullible.

The past fifty years have seen considerable scientific research on exceptional abilities. It is clear from this research that *some* people have *some* exceptional abilities *some* of the time. What is useful for us to realize is that *most* people (the rest of us!) have some of those abilities some of the time. Also, it turns out that some of these abilities can be trained (and improved) in the same way we might learn to play a musical instrument.

Have you ever thought about calling someone, and as your hand moved toward the phone, it rang? Who was calling? It was the person you were thinking of calling.

Have you ever talked about someone you haven't seen for years and the very next day you get a letter from that person?

Has anyone in your family ever had a dream, then found that the dream was true?

These are all common occurrences, examples of exceptional abilities which we have been told are out of our reach. By paying attention to those events, wouldn't it be something if we could develop them beyond our present limits?

## Unusual People

Some people can remember vast quantities of information. Arturo Toscanini could conduct entire symphonies from memory. James Farley, a politician, learned to recognize at least 20,000 people by name and face.

When he was five, Nicholas Birns could amuse and amaze his friends by telling them the day of the week for any date they asked. Squirming and giggling he would announce that April 2, 1947, was Wednesday, October 21, 1929, a Monday. He was right, and he didn't know how he did it.

I knew a reporter for *The New York Times*. He had the ability to recall almost everything he ever read. When asked to quote a poem or to recall from a book what some character said, he would close his eyes and begin reciting what he had read. Asked how he did it, he said, "I don't know. I just see the pages in my mind and read what's on it."

Zerah Colburn couldn't read ordinary numbers, but he could solve complicated mathematical problems in his head in a split second—at the age of five. In the early 1800s this unschooled boy from Cabot, Vermont, became the talk of Europe and America because of his mysterious gift for instant calculations.

According to *Vermont Life* magazine, when he had been at school for only six weeks, Zerah couldn't tell one figure from another, but he solved incredibly difficult math problems in a flash before legislators at the state capital, Montpelier.

In Portsmouth, New Hampshire, Zerah was asked what number multiplied by itself would yield 998,001. In less than four seconds he replied, "999." Correct!

His father took Zerah out of school in hopes his human computer son could make a fortune for the family. In 1812 (when he was eight), Zerah and his father went to Liverpool, England, where they received a royal reception from Princess Charlotte. Dukes, earls, and distinguished scholars paid one shilling each to test this amazing boy from the backwoods.

Zerah took England by storm. Asked to raise 8 to the sixteenth power, he quickly responded with the correct figure—281,474,976,710,656. Then he continued to astound his questioners with the square root of 106,929 and the cube root of 268,336,125. And he gave his answers even before his questioners could write down the numbers they were asking for.

Some tried to trick Zerah by asking him what two numbers, when multiplied together, make 36,083. Zerah shook his head and said there were none. (Mathematicians call this a prime number because it is divisible by no number except 1.)

No wonder Zerah was at last hired by the British Board of Longitude to compute in his head the positions and variations of the stars. Today this same job is handled by industrial-sized computers.

From time to time, someone appears today who is faster than a modern computer. Shakuntula Devi, an Indian woman, visited the United States in 1976. While doing a demonstration at George Washington University, she quickly answered questions like "What is 13 factorial? $(13 \times 12 \times 11 \times 10 \times 9 \ldots$ etc.)?" "6227020800." One of her unusual comments was "Never use commas. They'll only confuse you."

Asked why she was demonstrating these talents, she answered, "I want to restore faith in the human mind. We have too much dependence on machines."

We have grown to accept and use calculators in our mathematics, because we all "know" it is impossible to do large-scale multiplications or square roots in our heads. But is it?

The truth? There are many capacities open to us which we could learn to use if we wanted to. One way to shed our ideas about limits is to understand that we may be able to tap into capacities of an exceptional nature simply by learning how to develop them.

Now to some tools for increasing human capacity.

### Self-Concept—Your Limiting Factor

As you have seen, the major single factor limiting success and happiness is your self-concept.

A low self-concept does two things which work *against* you:

First, a low self-concept keeps you from learning how to succeed. If you think "I can't dance," then you will never give yourself the chance to learn. If you are forced to learn to dance, you will fight against it. A low self-concept means you won't let yourself feel successful as a dancer. Even if you learn the steps or the rhythm, you won't feel relaxed. No matter what people tell you, you won't be satisfied that you are really doing it right.

> "It is easier to teach a blind man to see than to teach success to a determined failure."

Second, a low self-concept keeps you from respecting yourself or even liking yourself very much. With a low self-concept, opportunities, challenges, experiences may be available but you won't take them. That sounds crazy (and it is) but here's how it works. If you don't like yourself, you will treat yourself just the way you would treat another person you don't like.

Imagine you have been given two tickets to a concert by your favorite group. Whom would you take? Someone you like or someone you don't like? Dumb question! Obviously you would take someone you like.

Now here's the application—just as you wouldn't take somebody you don't like to a pleasurable event, you might not give yourself opportunities to enjoy life. Sound absurd? Sure. But it actually may work this way.

Imagine you see someone you'd like to go out with. You say to yourself: "They would never go out with me. I'm too shy. Besides, I feel ugly. They'd go for a different type."

Now, what happens if this person, by some act of fate, wants to go out with you? What you will communicate is:

"I'm too shy for you."

"Haven't you noticed how unattractive I am?"

"You wouldn't really like me if you got to know me."

The result will be that the person you would like to go out with learns the truth—You don't feel you're worth much ... you don't think you're much fun to be with. So why should that person bother? They'll go along with your opinion and leave you alone!

## Your Self-Concept Was Fixed Until Now

We've looked at how you got your present self-concept:

a. Your parents told you what you should be like.

b. Your parents told you how you should behave.

c. Your parents told you that you were a winner.

d. Your parents told you that you were a loser.

Then, what your parents didn't tell you directly, you learned by imitating them or rebelling against them.

Maybe you talk like one parent or you enjoy certain activities your other parent likes. Or the reverse may be true. You say, "I'm exactly opposite of my mother."

## Can You Change?

Yes! You *can* change the way you think about yourself. You can change the way you are. It's not as difficult as it seems. You can do it by deciding to do it. You can become consciously aware of your old patterns and your old ways of keeping yourself limited. Then you can decide you don't want these negatives to control you any longer.

When you make that decision, you will be open to some exciting possibilities. Now real changes, solid changes, can occur in the directions you want to expand.

Because you are no longer a child, you have other ways besides your parents to get feedback about yourself. Most important, of course, is your own opinion of yourself. At first, however, that is hard to understand; it's based on all that old childhood stuff. Saying "I'm *not* clumsy!" to yourself will automatically lead to another voice inside you saying "Of course you're clumsy, and now you're crazy, too."

Simply saying to yourself that you are different won't

work at this stage. You need to see that the future is not as fixed as the past was for you.

## You and Your Friends

Take a long look at your friends. Look at them in a way you have never looked before. Ask yourself some questions about your relationships with them. Try these for starters:

Do my friends respect me?

Do my friends encourage me to improve?

Do my friends accept my failures and encourage me to accept them?

Are my friends the kind of people I respect?

Do my parents feel good about my friends?

    If so, why? What are they seeing?

    If not, why? What are they seeing?

You may find that you are not as impressed with some of your friends as you thought. That's not being disloyal; that's just starting to see that you have surrounded yourself with friends who both help and hinder your ability to change.

When I was a sophomore in college, I got into a whole dorm of guitar-players and folksingers. As the year unfolded, I found myself getting interested in the guitar (risky for me because "I couldn't play a tune on a comb!"). But with the help of my friends I actually bought a guitar and started to play.

My friends didn't assume that I had no talent; they only assumed I didn't know how to play yet! They supported me in changing my self-concept. They gave me help and advice, which made it easy for me to improve. My friends turned out to be the turning point for me. I realized that I really could change! Then and there, I started to be more than I ever thought I would be. You realize it would have taken only one or two people laughing at me for me to give up playing my guitar, to remain convinced that I could never play.

So, your friends can also be powerful forces in helping you to change. If you get the chance to change schools, it may be a rare opportunity for you to decide on who you really want to be. Your old patterns don't have to follow you to a new school. You can dress differently, talk differently, attract different people. You can do all these things, if you decide to. Sure, it's hard and lonely to change schools. But it can also mean an exciting new world for an exciting new year.

The first year of college often brings sweeping changes in people. They get the chance to be away from their families and old friends. They can try new things, discover new possibilities. Sometimes it doesn't work. Some college students get depressed and self-pitying. But these same feelings could lead to discovery of a new self.

## Why Bother Changing?

Is change really necessary? "What if I like myself the way I am? What's the big deal about improvement? Or personal growth? Self-concept? Isn't it just one more trip? After all, I'm getting by okay. Of course, I'm not great, but I'm good enough. Most people in the world aren't any happier than I am, so why all the fuss?"

When I began this chapter, I said I would offer you ways to help you succeed, if you wanted to. The question is "What's the payoff for being open and vulnerable? What do I gain by taking greater risks? Why should I change my self-concept from 'I can't' to 'I can'?"

Here are some answers worth thinking through:

1. The world is more satisfying if you're successful.
2. You get more out of life if you're not in a constant struggle to survive.

3. You can be of more service, more valuable and more helpful to others if you excel at whatever you do.

4. Winning is more fun than losing. You can have better grades, spend more time with fun people, win at sports, have a more interesting job.

Winning doesn't always mean beating somebody else. It may mean something inside you—a high self-concept. More satisfying, more pleasurable experiences. Everybody can win, including you!

Without tools, most of this chapter would be just another thinly disguised pilot of moral mouthings—"do well," "stay healthy," "get good grades," "be kind to little animals," and so on. So, here come the tools:

## Goal-Setting—Getting It All Laid Out

It is amazing how few people ever stop to consider what they want, to set goals. They drift along doing what is usual, getting by, being surprised by what happens. It is as if people let the world run by them. They let themselves be pulled from job to job, from home to home, from relationship to relationship. Like jellyfish on the beach, the waves throw them in and out with the tide.

Life doesn't need to be unplanned. There is an alternative. You can decide what you want to do, who you want to be, where you want to live, what kind of person you want to marry, what kind of job you would like to have. Deciding these things is the first and most important step in making them real.

We have seen that being called clumsy or artistic or selfish when you were young helped you to become those things. In the same way, seeing your own goals clearly can help you achieve them.

How can you clarify your goals? The best way is to write them down. Make a list of things you want—real things:
    a car
    an apartment
    a microscope
Include on your list personal goals, too:
    good grades
    clear skin
    making the tennis team
    being more confident
    being on time
What are the limits to your goals? How about deciding that you want $10,000,000? Or you want to be a rock star? Your limits are determined only by your willingness to believe in yourself. Can you hold in your mind a picture of yourself actually having that much money, that much fame? If that seems absolutely impossible for you, then make your goal within your own grasp; keep your goals realistic to you.

This exercise can be done again and again during your lifetime. As you reach your first goal, you can then extend your vision to include bigger, more challenging, more complex goals.

Let's say your field is music. Why not start with a goal of having your own band that plays at high school functions? Once you have that, write down new goals—a solid income from music, cutting your first record. That accomplished (and it may take you several years), you will be in a better position to shoot for even bigger goals. More money. Fame. In this way you will gradually see that the long-range goal, once far away, now seems like a genuine possibility.

Look at the list of goals you've made. Does it cover your needs? Health? Personal relationships? Self-respect? Being genuinely appreciated by others? Special skills? Things you'd like to own?

It's important to get your goals written as clearly as possible. Otherwise you won't be able to tell if you are making progress toward them or if you've achieved them. Be as specific as you can. "I want to do better in school" is too vague. How about "I want to get four A's next semester. I want an A in math, an A in psychology"?

Now you're getting explicit, and that's good.

## Visualizations

Visualizations are pictures you hold in your mind by using your imagination. They are helpful in changing your self-concept so that you can reach your goals more easily.

Let me show you what visualization is like:

Close your eyes for a moment and imagine that you are up in the mountains on a beautiful day taking a hike. Feel the dirt under your boots. Smell the air. Feel yourself enjoying the walk. See the view around you.

You have just given yourself a pleasant imaginary experience. When you imagine an experience like this you can actually *feel* as if you are there in the mountains. When you open your eyes, you may feel refreshed and relaxed. What you are doing is training your mind to have the kinds of experiences you want. By imagining positive experiences, you can cause them to come true.

A visualization is a mental experience, as vivid as you'd like to make it to help your mind accept new behaviors which you'd like to have.

Example:

Let's assume one of your goals is to get an A on your next exam. Your mind has collected all the instances of your life when you've had to take an exam—some good, some not so good. Your past experience in test-taking will influence how you do on your next exam. If you have usually been tense (or grumpy or tired) before an exam, it's likely you will be that way before the next one.

Now you're going to change those habits. You sit quietly and imagine yourself taking the test. You imagine yourself feeling confident, smiling. You understand the materials and are prepared (even if you don't understand it all, imagine you do!). You imagine that you are relaxed while you're working. You don't feel rushed or pressured. You imagine completing the test, feeling satisfied, proud of yourself as you turn it in. You imagine leaving the room refreshed, humming your favorite tune.

A fantasy? No! This is visualization which has helped train your mind to let you succeed. You can make this visualization come true, whereas most of our fantasies border on the "impossible."

You may find at first that your mind will not do what you wish. For example, when you imagine trying to run a perfect race, all kinds of strange events may occur. You may see yourself tripping. You may find a puddle of water on the track. You may even forget which direction to go.

It may surprise you to find that your mind won't always do what you wish. The reason is that your mind is programmed by old habits. It resists change. At first it resists any change. But once you get your mind in gear, you will find that your body actually follows the track laid down by your visualization. Then your performance improves.

Now another good thing happens. When you can easily visualize winning, you will automatically listen more to coaching. You may find yourself putting out more during workouts, and you may even note that you're eating better, and all of this to help your body get into better shape.

"Can this really work?" Great athletes attribute their success in part to their tremendous ability to concentrate and "visualize" themselves winning. Many successful people "saw" their success before it became reality.

What you're doing when you visualize is making your mind open and responsive to achieving your goals. Do you want your skin to clear up? Visualize yourself with clear skin. Overhear someone saying "I wish I had skin like that." Think of someone special running a hand over your face.

Daily visualization trains your mind to direct you toward your goals—*no matter what your previous beliefs or experiences have been!*

Now you have your goals and you have a way of sensitizing your mind to the possibility of achieving them. There is another way to make it all happen still faster.

## Affirmations

An affirmation is a positive statement about yourself. It is another way of conditioning your mind to get out of old habits and into new ones.

Your brain has two sides. One side handles verbal material; it deals with speaking, writing, mathematics, logic. The other side of your brain works with visual data; it deals with images, music, physical activities. Example? You can easily ride a bike. But you may find it hard to describe the details in words. Your visualizations are working with one side of your brain—the visual side. Affirmation uses words to open up the other side.

And you can make up an affirmation about any of your goals.

Suppose your goal is to be a good dancer. Your visualization might be to see yourself dancing with great skill and ease. People are watching you with admiration and you feel good. That's visualization. Now the affirmation might be "I am an excellent dancer. I enjoy myself at every dance."

"Wait a minute," you argue. "This was making sense for a while. It even sounded encouraging. But I can't dance and I never have been able to. Do you expect me to believe that by saying a few magic words my problems will disappear like smoke?"

No, I don't think they will go like smoke. This is like chipping away at a block of wood. Inside the wood there is a statue of a fine dancer. Right now it's blocked from view by all those past embarrassing experiences. Each time you visualize, each time you affirm, you chip away at the old image. Gradually you bring out a new you. This new you enjoys dancing.

A friend of mine grew up convinced that he had no musical skill. He'd taken lessons when he was a child, but his family had let him know that he was "the worst piano-player in the family." They loved him, but they didn't understand that a remark like that would drive anyone away from the piano. As a teenager he was so piano-shy, so musically inhibited, that if he entered a room with a piano, he unknowingly placed himself as far from it as possible.

Then he learned about goals and affirmation. He decided to visualize that he was capable of playing music. All this time he kept telling himself that he was a good musician. He took up guitar a few months later and within three years was able to take part in a master's class for classical guitar. Once he stopped telling himself how bad he was, he could expand his self-concept and he became a musician.

Sure, there is a limit to all this. But the limit is how willing you are to let yourself be happy; to let yourself be successful; to let yourself be popular; to work toward your goal.

There is still another way of helping yourself toward any goal. This is to like yourself more and more and more. We're not talking about conceit. Conceit is trying to make others like you because you really don't know if you're worth liking. What we are talking about is genuine liking. Liking yourself, feeling about yourself the way you feel about people you love.

## Review

If you've been trained to believe you're not worth liking, you can reverse that training. You can retrain your mind to improve your overall opinion of yourself.

How:

   *Set a goal*—feeling better about yourself.

   *Visualization*—see yourself happy, confident, getting an award, looking at an all-A report card, winning a race, being hugged.

   *Affirmation*—say a sentence that is like your visualization, such as "I won the race." "I enjoy being hugged."

   Say the words "I like myself." Say them again, and again.

Too simple? No, because it works, and it makes sense. It works because you have been doing something like it most of your life. Since you were little your parents helped you set goals. Some good, some bad:

"You'll never be as smart as your sister." "You're a mess." "You have got a talent for picking the wrong friends." "You can win." "You're a brain."

You've also lived by affirmation, by visualizations, by imagining and dreaming.

So you see, you've been doing everything I've laid out already, and doing it well. These suggestions are simply to go on doing what you've been doing, only now you are going to take control of your life. You're deciding how things will go.

Once your decisions are clear, you can use the tools you've always had. The results will come as they have always come. But there is one big difference. Now you can get the results you want instead of the results programmed into you years ago.

I know a woman who had a cancer. She was in therapy,

and the therapy was making her almost as sick as the cancer. She finally said to her doctor that she couldn't bear the therapy and she'd just as soon die of cancer as of the treatment for it. She stopped treatment and returned home. Her doctor told her she was committing suicide and he could not be held responsible. Once home, she began *affirming* that she was healthy; she *visualized* herself as healthy; and she did return to health; her cancer shrank to a little scar tissue. She then realized how much more she could do with her life. She returned to school, received an advanced degree and is now an important teacher in the local college.

Another man I know decided at age thirty-four to make huge amounts of money. By age thirty-six he had gone into real estate and had actually made several million dollars. He also found he didn't enjoy his work so he sold out and retired at thirty-six, able to do whatever he chose.

A woman from Dallas, Texas, who lost her leg as a child in an auto accident, plans to fly in the cross-country Powder Puff Derby. "I know what I am" was her response when asked how she could fly an airplane without legs.

Through her courage and persistence, she was issued a pilot's license—the first ever granted to a handicapped person. She was nineteen years old at the time. As if flying an airplane weren't enough, she also swims, surfs, and rides a motorcycle. Her legs were amputated at the hips and she "walks" on her hands.

Lisa decided to stop biting her nails. I saw it happen. She wrote down the goal, visualized herself with long nails, said to herself, "I am not a nailbiter." Two weeks later she showed up in my class, held up her hands for everyone to see, and told us it worked.

With all of these people, "visualizing" had worked quickly. The first time they visualized and affirmed, they stopped some of their old habits. The old versions of themselves were ready to go. A very small push was all it took.

---

You may feel a little like Tina and Gary did after they finished reading this chapter. Here are their reactions:

GARY:   This sounds like it gives us false hopes. Are you saying if I visualize clear skin my face will clear up? It seems misleading to me.

TINA:   It's not all this easy. Maybe for some people this works, but not for me! It's too simple to just say "You can if you want to."

It may really seem impossible that we can be changed by how we think. This may all appear to be saying "Pull yourself up by the bootstraps." But it's much deeper than that. It involves a commitment to a goal and a willingness to be more than you are. For Gary, the commitment may also involve a change in diet as a part of his visualization. And for Tina, it may involve a change in how she sees herself.

You are capable of being what you want. It may be easy, it may be difficult. But it *is* possible. If you're willing to grow, you are on the right track to making it happen.*

*This material is derived from the work of John Boyle and the Institute of Executive Research, Glendale, California.

# MYRTLE T. COLLINS

Myrtle Telleen Collins received her B.A. in speech and English at the University of Northern Iowa, Cedar Falls, Iowa, and her M.A. in counseling and guidance at Colorado College, Colorado Springs, Colorado.

She has had experience as a teacher of English, drama, remedial reading, and social studies on the junior high and senior high levels; teacher of elementary grades, dean of girls in a junior high, counselor on all levels; principal of an American school abroad (Vientiane, Laos); coordinator of student teaching at the University of Hawaii, and coordinator of a federally funded project on mainstreaming the mildly handicapped, also at the University of Hawaii.

She is the author of several professional articles published in journals of educational psychology and teaching. With her husband, Dwane R. Collins, she co-authored the book, *Survival Kit for Teachers (and Parents)*, published by Goodyear Publishing Company.

# *You and Your Friends*

Did you ever let a friend down? Bothered you, didn't it? It bothered Tom, too.

Football practice was over and he dragged into the house. Heading for the shower, he told his mother, "It's been a bad day, please don't bother me." So wouldn't you know? Halfway through he heard her calling. "Tom! The phone ... for you."

"Tell him I can't talk now!" he yelled. Then he finished his shower and dropped on the bed. Almost asleep, he heard her again. "Tom, Tom! It's Steve... the second time he's called."

Next day the entire community knew about Steve's dad. There'd been a terrible accident. Mr. Johnson was dead. Steve Johnson was Tom's best friend. What do you do when your best friend's father is killed in an accident? And what do you do when everyone is saying "If the doctor had come in time, he might have made it?"

That's why Steve had been calling Tom! The doctor's car had stalled, and when Steve finally found someone who could bring the doctor, it was too late.

So that's how it was. Steve had tried to call Tom first. There is only one word to describe how Tom felt now— awful. All day, all night, Tom thought about letting his friend down. Sometimes he would break out in a cold sweat. Sometimes he shivered. Sometimes he dreamed bad dreams.

The story you have read is true. Where it happened doesn't matter, because it could have happened anywhere, to anyone.

Who do you suppose finally brought Tom out of it? You guessed it—Steve. Isn't it something when the friend you're most worried about is the person who helps you put the unchangeable behind you? Small wonder Tom thinks Steve is the greatest.

Friendship is on the minds of everybody from kindergarten to the grave. One study of more than 3000 high school students shows clearly that friendship is the number-one concern.

What exactly is friendship? What does it mean? Let's take a closer look.

## The Nature of Friendship

First, friendship is a basic human need. Without it we are afraid. Experts say we never really get over this fear unless we are understood by at least one other person. They also tell us that relating to another person is essential to our growth.

Friendship is loaded with responsibility. What A can require of B, B may expect from A. "If you'll like and accept me as I am, I will do the same for you." Fair trade. Freeing and demanding.

It's never static, but fluid, on the move. Flowing like a river. Good friendships maintain a certain sameness, yet every moment is new.

Friendships can be very fragile, too. We humans are tender. Unlike the armadillo, we have no heavy external protection when it comes to forming friendships. We must rely on our wits, our instincts, and our preferences. Some friendships develop cracks. Before we realize it, there is a broken relationship. Sometimes, though, fractured friendships can be patched and made stronger than ever. So friendship is a demanding, ongoing relationship, cracks, breaks, and all.

By some, friendship is called a great social game that requires at least two qualified players. Would it surprise you to know that there are some who just can't play, the reason being that they are so sensitive to being hurt they can't stand friendship. It's true. Or can you imagine being called unfit for friendship? Unfit to be an astronaut, perhaps, or a brain surgeon—but friendship? Some people make poor friends because they are totally insensitive to the needs of others. These people are all wrapped up in themselves like small packages. They haven't yet learned to share.

Friendship is a feeling. A special one that turns you on,

gives you a sense of pride and sharing. Without it you're a dud; with it you're alive. Some call that certain feeling "spiritual"—something beyond the understanding of the normal Earthling. Call it "that certain something," "a gift of love." Whatever you name it, you *feel* it.

Friendship offers opportunities to expand your acquaintances, to recognize those certain feelings inside you and to learn how to handle them. Call them hungers, juices, passions, label them as you will; whatever they are, they need some management. Now is the best time to get them under control, and that doesn't mean squelching. Far from it. It means getting to know your emotional drives.

This is an ongoing and sometimes large task. Two things can give you encouragement: (1) You *can* learn ways of coping with your own feelings. (2) Remember, your peers are struggling with the same problems.

### Escaping Loneliness

Stephanie was one of the best-liked girls I ever knew. Whenever there was an election, the question was, "Who will be elected besides Stephanie?"

You wouldn't know it from looking at her. She was really quite plain. Hornrimmed glasses. Thin. But everybody loved Stephanie. One day I asked her, "Steffie, how do you do it?"

"Well," she replied, "I guess it's because I remember something my grandmother taught me. What she said was 'Never forget, Steffie, everybody is a little bit lonesome."

—*Dr. Charlie Shedd*

Friendship is a means of escaping loneliness. Everyone's lonely sometimes. Some more than others, or maybe some just show it more. You know the deep-down sick feeling when everyone but you seems to be having fun. And the sudden relief when someone pays attention to you! The rescuer seems too good to be true. There you were, ready to sneak out and never, never show up at another party, when presto, everything changed.

At times like that just about *anybody* reaching out can become overly important to you. If you haven't thought about this possibility you could get hurt. When you feel lonely, your judgment may not be the best. Instant buddies can sometimes be like instant anything—a good imitation, extra sweet, not very nourishing, and often not all that good for you.

Friendship involves risk. This is true because all of us are on a constant hunt for others who will accept our secret selves. We go looking for those who can even stand our ugliness, the rough unfinished part of us. Of course, we take chances when we expose ourselves. But one who accepts our exposure, who doesn't withdraw from it, is a candidate for friendship.

In seeking friendship we make ourselves vulnerable. We can be badly hurt, double-crossed, even feel like we've been destroyed. It's a sobering thought, but one that ought to be remembered. If we use our heads, we can even learn from the experience we first called failure.

## Choices

Friendship is also a matter of choice. Remember those emotion-packed moments of choosing up sides for a ball game? Selecting friends is something like that. Sure, the best players will be chosen first. But why did all those others come before you? The reasons aren't always clear.

Research shows that we single out favorites for one or more of the following reasons:

The person (1) supports our ideas (about government, family, sex, and so on); (2) satisfies a material need (money, car, movie passes); (3) meets an emotional need (physical contact). Ideas... things... feelings. The friends you choose in response to those strong forces will affect your future. They will affect your goals. They will influence the way you meet success and failure. They will gauge the fun you get out of being you.

Serious choices always carry responsibility and restriction. Deciding on one friend, or set of friends, can exclude others from your life. Every choice involves some restrictions. We can't have everything and we can't be a friend to everyone. No one has the time, interest, or energy to be everyone's good friend. So choosing involves conscious decisions as well as emotional vibrations, and very often these conscious thoughts can be our best guide. We choose on instinct and thought. Sure, there are other reasons for selections. But the point is that there are rational and irrational components to the choices we make.

The above statements are only a few observations of the nature of friendship, but they confirm the fact that friendship is indeed serious business for all of us.

## Seeking and Finding Friends

In seeking companions, as in any other conscious effort, we can use several aids. Hunches. Logic. Horse sense. If we use them all, we may be in for some happy surprises. Like Prince Charming, we may search in far countries, only to find the Princess next door. Such are the mysteries of life, full of "what if's," "might have's," and "wow's!"

Rate by number the qualities you want in a friend (from one to ten, ten being the best or highest score):

| _____ disposition | _____ sensitivity |
| _____ intelligence | _____ personality |
| _____ looks | _____ money |
| _____ common interests | _____ humor |
| _____ fun | _____ easy to talk with |
| _____ abilities | |

## Identity Clarification

What draws people together? You may have noticed how human beings often bunch together according to color, size, shape. That's "identity clarification." We all do it. We need to see ourselves, and one way we see ourselves is through someone like us. It's like looking in a mirror. We think, "You're neat; I'm like you. Therefore I'm neat, too." Simple equation. Logical and reassuring.

Similarities do draw people together initially. Our first friends were from our neighborhood, the club, church, or school.

Later, this mirroring takes on larger proportions. Then the attractiveness of *dissimilarity* begins. Differences may even become the glue holding friends together. Now the choice has more to do with personality than factors like money, religion, or nationality.

Traditionally, girls tend to "mirror" more than boys. Boys often make fewer demands regarding closeness. Girls are more often accused of being snobbish or cliquish. Boys usually feel common interests like boats, cards, or athletics are more important. But in a changing world, these stereotypes can often be wrong. The important thing is to take each person for what he or she is and make decisions based on your experience—not on traditional role assumptions.

## Peer Group Pressure

PGP (peer group pressure) is a powerful influence at any age, but particularly during the teens. If you stop to think about these behaviors you may decide you're living in a pressure chamber.

Some parents are threatened by the strong PGP force in your life. They may have forgotten your need for a neutral field to work out your feelings. Or they don't remember the need for friends as listeners, mirrors, models. It's a good idea, if this happens, to try understanding their sense of rejection. If they didn't care, they wouldn't even bother to react. But someway they must come to understand. It is natural for you to change your preferences and to look outside the home or neighborhood for new friendships.

"My parents and I are having a bad time. They have always told me I couldn't date anyone older than I am. Well, I have met this boy who is in the service, stationed at the naval base in our town. He is the nicest guy I've ever met. He treats me like no one else ever treated me. But he is four years older than I am and my parents don't want me to see him. They don't want him to come over. And they don't want me going anywhere with him. Don't you think they are being unreasonable? I also want to know: Do parents have the right to tell you who you can be friends with?"

—*From a high school girl*

What would you tell her?

If you're serious about finding good friends, you'll seek out groups which share your interest: music, drama, animals, hiking, sports, or whatever it may be. Have you ever hidden behind the old excuse "But I never know what to talk about?" Maybe you need to go where people like what you like, where you will be able to find a common ground.

The main word is *action* ... act ... move ... don't just sit there. Others might, or might not, come to you. Other people are timid, too. So you're one giant step ahead if you're *rational*. You've thought it through and you understand your objective. You're on a purposeful search for friends. If you meet some rejection, move on. If you stay with it, someone is bound to respond.

## Signs of a Genuine Friendship

Some friends are closer than others. While acquaintances or casual friends are important, close friends are the ones who generally mean the most. You can share the most of yourself with them and not worry about being judged for what you feel or think. What are the marks of a genuine friendship? Here are seven signs of a good thing going:

SIGN ONE. When you meet a real friend you feel *equal* in some special way. This may not always be true intellectually or socially, but some way you feel equal. This makes you comfortable with each other.

SIGN TWO. *Trust* is added to your equality. You can afford to be honest with each other because you have a mutual trust. Confidences will be shared and secrets kept.

SIGN THREE. *Spontaneity* marks a real friendship. Listen to good friends when they're together. "Umm hm," "Yeah," "Nah." Maybe it's only a subvocal murmur, but volumes are spoken, understood. Some things you say would make the outsider wince, but you know they're said with a special affection. There is spontaneity here. This is good humor, fun for two.

SIGN FOUR. Good friendship is measured by *time-quality*, not quantity. Did you ever meet a friend after a long separation, and you were surprised? Surprised that you picked up right where you left off? Time may have separated you, but couldn't separate your feelings about each other.

SIGN FIVE. Good friendships lack *stress*. That's not to say you don't disagree about things, but being together is natural, comfortable. Like gliding. There's no need to explain or apologize.

SIGN SIX. Good friends are not afraid of *silence*. Among strangers silence can be deafening. With someone close, there are fewer worries. No need to fill the air with mindless chatter. Secrets from each other are okay for a while. So is privacy. So is aloneness sometimes. Friends understand the need for quiet.

SIGN SEVEN. Friends share values. Sure, your values will vary, but you will be free to talk about anything. Even though you may hold very different views, no subject is taboo.

Having cited the signs of a genuine friendship, it seems only reasonable to mention an important caution factor: motive. Motives in friendships bear watching. We have said that personalities and common interests are the two strongest binders in friendship. But there are some strong, less admirable reasons for one person choosing another. For example, do you know a pair in which a "weak" character sticks to a "strong" one? ("Be my slave and you can go around with me.") Such alliances come under the heading *Used*. Choosing friends for financial, social, or dependency is courting disappointment.

Good friendships make each person better. But there are relationships that can be harmful to those involved. This can happen in friendship and we need to be alert to it. Friendships nurtured by purely selfish or unworthy goals (neurotic behavior) keep us from being our best.

## Terminating Friendships

Like plants, some friendships die. One reason is the transplanting which takes place in our mobile society. The average American moves fifteen times in one lifetime. Uprooting is hard on good friends, especially teenagers. Few are able to handle it with ease.

Some friendships are terminated because they should be. Neither person is benefiting. Or one "friend" is always "winning" and the other "losing." Other friendships move into the disaster area because they push too fast. Telling too much too soon can sometimes be deadly. Fear of what the other might say can cause anxiety. Values change; preferences, likes, and dislikes change. There are many reasons why friendships fade in and out. And this is probably good. Most of us can handle many casual acquaintances, but only a few close ones.

## Keeping the Friendship Going

In the glow of a developing friendship or the misery of a broken one, one question may recur: How can I keep my friendships growing? Here are some ideas, questions, suggestions, and a place for you to check your first, second, and third choices.

1. Apology (How should I apologize?)
   a. Swallow my pride? _____
   b. Try a simple "I'm sorry"? _____
   c. Write a note? _____
   d. Send a message through a mutual friend? _____
   e. Other. _____

2. Compliments (How should I pay my friend a compliment?)
   a. Tell them when I think of it? _____
   b. Wait a while to be sure? _____
   c. Tell another mutual friend? _____
   d. Other. _____
3. Advice (How should I advise a friend?)
   a. Help them see the options? _____
   b. Kid a bit? _____
   c. Tell them about someone else I know? _____
   d. Be prepared for my advice to be ignored? _____
   e. Be frank but not rude? _____ ("Don't be stupid" can be replaced with "Here's another way to think about it."
   f. Other. _____
4. Jealousy (How can I cope with jealousy in myself and others?)
   a. Understand that jealous people feel inferior and are in the habit of denying their feelings? _____
   b. Talk about it? _____
   c. Tell them to go see a professional? _____
   d. Other. _____
5. Competition (How should I deal with competition?)
   a. Talk about it honestly? _____
   b. Examine my own values? _____ (Do I really care?)
   c. Ask myself and my friend "Why do we have this 'I've got to win' feeling"? _____
   d. Other. _____
6. Communication (How can I communicate better with my friends?)
   a. Write to those far away? _____
   b. Telephone? _____
   c. Cultivate a thoughtful attitude? _____
   d. Be attentive? _____

e. Respect their privacy? _____ ("If this is not a good time to talk, call me back.")

f. I will not assume that friendship gives me ready access to my friends' time and privacy. I will be courteous. _____

g. Other. _____

7. Loyalty and trust (How can my friend and I build loyalty and trust?)

a. By being willing to reveal ourselves? _____

b. By never talking behind backs? _____

c. By keeping secrets? _____ (Remember I do not have the right to decide when a secret is "not worth keeping" or "too good to keep.")

d. Other. _____

8. "No" (Is it possible to learn to say no to my friends?)

a. I will rehearse "No" in my mind for certain situations. _____

b. When peer pressure forces me to say "Yes" but I prefer to say "No," I will talk it over with someone. _____

c. Things I would say "No" to are:

_____

_____

_____

> "I'm going to do whatever I want, and no one's going to stop me. This is a free society, so why not? I'm not talking about murdering someone, you know, but I've got my freedom to do anything. I'm just going to do my thing, and if it bothers you, tough luck, mister."
> —*A high school boy*

"When I say I want to do my own thing, I'm on dangerous territory unless I remember this: everyone else has a thing to do too. It is evil for me to do my thing if it encroaches on other people's rights. Their rights are as precious to them as mine are to me. They feel the urge to be what they think they should be. The entire business of my rights must be understood against the background of everyone else's rights too."
—*Charlie Shedd, "Strictly for Dads"*

Discuss these two views and try to arrive at your own philosophy.

## Questions

1. *What if no one wants to be my friend?*

   Try developing an interest you enjoy doing alone. Then ask one person to join you. Eventually you may collect a group.

2. *Is it harder for gifted teenagers to make friends?*
   Yes. This may be true for several reasons. One is the envy factor. The gifted, like anyone else, must sort values and select or be selected on the basis of mutual attractiveness. Every human being has some gift to share.

3. *Is there any basic friendship advice?*

   Yes. Make new acquaintances continuously, and with all age groups. Keep those relationships in good repair. Then when you lose someone through death, geographical separation, or loss of interest, there will be others to fill the void.

4. *Can I avoid friendship problems?*

No. As we have noted, there are friendship skills just as there are reading and writing skills. Mastering friendship is no snap. The strength and tensile of a deep relationship do not depend on "no strain." Difficulties and problems faced together can help us grow.

5. *I have heard it said "Your husband, your wife can be your best friend." Is that true?*

Why not? Do you know any couples who look and act like best friends? _____

6. *What's the final word?*

"First to thine own self be true." Strive to find yourself fit company for you. Begin by being glad you're male or female. Beyond that, be glad you're a human being with a capacity for reaching out to another... and another. In friendship you are enfolding and freeing someone else to be whole. That concept holds the hope of a friendlier world.

# CHARLIE W. SHEDD

Dr. Shedd's straightforward, witty advice on everything from teen sex to family democracy has been enjoyed and put into practice by millions of people. Through the impact of his lecture tours and best-selling books (*Letters to Karen, Letters to Phillip, The Stork Is Dead*), Dr. Shedd makes people laugh, respond, and—most important—make changes in their lives.

Dr. Shedd is well known among young people for his sometimes startling, always straight-from-the-shoulder column in *Teen Magazine*, "Sex and Dating." During the four years when this column was regularly featured in *Teen*, he received more than 25,000 letters from teenagers across the nation with questions covering the entire gamut of youthful concerns.

Dr. Shedd has made appearances on national talk shows, been featured in an NBC special, and is presently heard on many radio stations across the country in his syndicated "Parent Talk" broadcasts.

# You and Your Family

Have you ever been in a helicopter? It's a fun ride, slow and low. Slow enough to see things you can't see from a fast plane. Low enough to pick up other details you might miss from the ground.

This chapter will be a helicopter ride over your family: their oddities, emotions, hurts, and even some good things.

This year can be a training lab in how to blend. It can also teach you how to manage when you can't blend. I know teenagers who operate on the thought "When I get away from home, then I can live exactly the way I want, do what I want, say what I want, be me."

It's probably not that simple. Anyplace you go, anything you do, you're sure to meet people. People who are easy to live with as well as difficult people. Gentle folks, toughies, and kooks. You may also have a boss who says "Do it my way," even though you know your way would be better. In one sense, it's an ugly world. And should you approach it looking for trouble, you'll find it. But it can also be a beautiful world, with interesting people and fascinating happenings. And how beautiful it is for you depends in part on how well you have learned to relate at home.

Since that's where you're probably still living, the time is right for looking at how you relate at home. Here are some ideas for thinking through.

Section I presents points for discussion.

Section II is the report of unusual things which have worked in some families.

Section III is a set of suggestions on how to get along with your parents.

### SECTION I
### *The Problems of Family Life*

#### "DADDY, YOU LEFT THE DOOR OPEN"

Many of the letters I receive are full of complaints: "I don't like what's going on around here." But now and then I get one like this:

My husband is a doctor and life hasn't always been easy for us. But recently something happened I want to share with you.

Like most families we have certain unwritten laws which everyone is expected to follow. One of these rules is about our garage door. The last person going to bed is to lock it, and there are no excuses. There has been a great deal of theft in our neighborhood and our garage might be particularly tempting because of the power tools. My husband is a hobby craftsman.

One morning recently he woke up early as usual and went to get the paper. There was the garage door wide open. It wasn't the first time, of course, and he has a regular lecture for these occasions. But this morning he had just gotten started when Beth (she's in high school) stopped him in his tracks with her own lecture.

"Daddy, you left the garage door open. I know you had to be the one because I stayed up late studying and I certainly locked it when I went to bed. Who else could have done it? Since you weren't home yet, it had to be you! And just in case you wondered, some of us around here have had about all we can take being blamed for things we didn't do!"

> Have you ever talked to your father this way? If not, could you? What do you think Beth's father should do?

That night at dinner Beth's father apologized. He said, "I admit I had it coming, Beth. I really did, and I want to tell you I'm sorry."

> Why don't we hear more notes of apology in the family? When some-

one does apologize to us, do we tend to think less of them? Or more? How long has it been since you said "I'm sorry" at home?

### A FATHER CHANGES HIS MIND

Heather is a high school senior. She works for her father each summer as a receptionist. He says she's very good, does an excellent job on the telephone and typewriter, but is especially good with people. Heather even keeps some of his personal records. She takes the place of a regular employee.

Only her father has a rather unusual quirk. He does not believe in paying his own children. He says, "They work for me. I give them room and board, buy their clothes, pay their way through college. What could be fairer than that?"

Do you think Heather's father has a legitimate point of view? If you were Heather, what would you do? Would you go along with your dad? Would you make a different proposition? If so, what?

It bothered Heather to ask for money, so she went straight to her dad and told him it was time to rethink the situation. This year she wanted a different deal. He said it again: "But I don't believe in putting my children on salary. I've never done it. Nobody in our family has ever done it. Why should we change now?"

He shouldn't have asked it, because Heather had a logical, reasoned response: "Dad, I think you're only burning incense to the past. Why follow an old family tradition that ought be dropped right here?"

Then she offered her proposal. "Tell you what. This year, why don't you figure my time at regular rates? You put half of it in the bank for my education and give me the other half to buy what you would be buying for me anyway. What could be fairer than that? It wouldn't cost you one cent more than the way you're doing it. Besides, I would get all that experience in handling money. You could watch and see how I do. Think how much better you'd feel when I go away to college."

### HOW MUCH LIBERTY?

Here are two letters from opposite ends of the discipline spectrum.

Dear Dr. Shedd:
Do you think it's possible for a girl to be unhappy because she can do anything she wants? My parents never ground me like my friends get grounded. They never say "No" about anything. Most of my friends think I'm lucky. But sometimes it scares me to be able to go anywhere and do everything with no one telling me when to stop.

Now here's a boy weary with dictatorship:

Dear Dr. Shedd:
Do you know how terrible it is to live with a father who is always right? My dad thinks he is like Jesus Christ, but I think he is more like Hitler. All of us kids hate him. And do you know what I think? I think my mom does too. It seems like a lot of my friends have the same problem. Believe me, next year when I go away to college, I'm going to let it all hang out.

How much authority is right? Are there different needs in different homes? Do you think your parents are too strict? Not strict enough? If you were to take these two letters home and read them at the dinner table, what reaction would you get? At your house what changes could be made to make things better?

## THE BLUE-JEAN WEDDING

Alice is being married in a big church wedding. She will wear the traditional wedding gown; her bridesmaids will wear similar dresses, too. But the groom has made an unusual announcement. He says he and his groomsmen will wear clean blue jeans and jean jackets, without ties.

The wedding is to be held in a fashionable church. Not stuffy, but dignified. And Alice's father says he won't pay for the wedding if the boys wear blue jeans.

Alice is putting pressure on her dad to accept the situation. She says, "But don't you believe in everyone doing his own thing?"

This dad is no old fogey. He takes plenty of time for his family, serves on the church board, and really believes what he believes. Now he's refusing to give an inch. No way will he pay the bill if the boys wear blue jeans.

Who's right? The boy she's marrying? Her dad? How far should young people go in expressing their individuality? How much do other people's feelings matter? Should a father use his money as a lever?

In reply to Alice's "Don't you believe in everybody doing his own thing," her dad answers, "You bet I believe in everyone doing his own thing. It's one of my basic beliefs. In fact, I believe in it so much that I believe in me doing my own thing. And my thing is not to pay for anything that would be embarrassing."

> If you were Alice's father and you felt blue jeans would be embarrassing, what would you do? Can you think of some alternatives? A compromise?

### "I TOLD YOU SO"

Nomination for the world's biggest bore: the person who is forever saying, *I told you so*. "Turned out just like I said it would, didn't it?" ... "You heard me say I didn't think it was a good idea." ... "If only you had listened."

> Are your parents like this? Are you?

Some people know when to keep their mouths shut. Here's a report from Scott:

"Last spring when I graduated from high school, I bought a motorcycle. My folks didn't like it. But they are the kind who said since I was through school, I could decide things like that myself. I'd been working since I was in junior high, so I had the money. I went ahead and spent it. Right away I took off from California just to see the country. Before I got there, I had a wreck in Arizona. I totaled the motorcycle, but I guess I was lucky because I was only in the hospital three days. My dad got off work and drove all the way from Michigan to bring me home. My mother has a job too, but she couldn't leave hers.

"What I want to tell you is that all the way back, my dad never once said anything about why I didn't take their advice. They never said anything like that when I got home either, and they haven't since. I think that is pretty great. And so do my friends, because when I tell them about it, they can hardly believe it."

Which one of these statements do you think most accurately sums up the situation? Why?

1. Scott's parents made a mistake by letting him buy the motorcycle. The accident was really their fault.

2. Scott went against his parents' wishes and because his father didn't say anything, Scott is likely to do it again.

3. By saying nothing, Scott's dad was really saying, "I extend you the dignity of learning some things on your own."

4. Because Scott's family treated him this way, Scott will have a new respect for them and he will really care more what they think.

### TELEPHONE RULES

The telephone can be a problem. But here's one family who turned potential trouble into a good thing. Recently, while I was in their home, an interesting scene took place.

We were sitting by the fire deep in conversation when their fourteen-year-old daughter came into the room. She excused herself for interrupting and then said, "Dad, I've got to make a telephone call. This one will take a while.

Do you have any important calls coming in?" When her father had given her the green light, she thanked him and disappeared. I thought that was something special, so I said, "You've got a winner there." To which her dad replied, "Thanks. But actually, it's all part of our deal. The telephone used to bug us. So we had some discussions and decided on a few rules."

When I asked him to tell me more, he continued. "In this telephone discussion everybody had his say, and one thing we agreed was that we'd check with each other before a long call." This man is a salesman and he gets a lot of his orders by phone at home. So misuse of the phone could have been big trouble, but they handled it by (1) some agreements ahead of time, and (2) the whole family working it out together.

They're using what could be trouble to bring them closer to each other.

> What problem areas at your house could you manage better by some agreements?

## HOW MUCH SHOULD A PARENT HELP WITH THE HOMEWORK?

Here's a parent writing his confessional to me. His daughter won first prize in this year's Science Fair. She entered some kind of miniature computer and it must have been very well made. From the way he describes the competition, it had to be good. Only now the whole thing has been getting to him. Here's one paragraph from his letter:

> This morning while I was reading the paper over coffee, I suddenly had this strange feeling. There was another scandal in our state government, and I was reading my

favorite editorial column. The writer was musing on dishonesty and saying that it can often be traced to something way back in a person's history. So his contention was that cheating could be the product of bad training in childhood. That's when it hit me. That Science Fair thing was strictly no good. I built that phony computer for my daughter. What am I teaching her? How to get by? How to win at any price? I talked it over with this friend of mine. He says to forget it. But it still bothers me.

> Do you think this father should be bothered? Is there too much pressure in your school? What should a parent do about homework, special projects, competition?

A friend of mine teaches high school physics. He's been leading a crusade to do away with what he calls "all competition which becomes a substitute for learning." Here's a part of his argument before the school authorities:

"The dullest boy in my class won first prize for his perpetual-motion machine. It really was a classic. I couldn't believe his father was that smart either. So I did some checking and here's what I found. They paid a graduate engineering student to make it for them. Now what's any high school student going to learn from that except how to cheat and get away with it? He has already learned that his family approves of cheating, that 'money talks,' and that winning is all important."

That's a good question. So my friend is beating a loud drum. He's against any kind of school contest where kids can enlist parents to compete, family against family. He says he wouldn't be so upset about it if it were out in the open. It's the sneaky stuff he doesn't like.

How do you feel?

This is what one family with five children did. They discussed it and agreed that Mom and Dad would help with the homework on this basis: "You tell your teacher that you and your parents are working together. If it's okay with the school, it's okay with us."

### BICYCLE GENIUS

Dennis is a genius at fixing bicycles. He has always been a mechanical whiz. In second grade, some of his best friends were working for A's. But not Dennis. He was taking his bicycle apart and putting it back together. By junior high, his mind was constantly turning over with wheels, sprockets, hand brakes, and ten-speed drives. During his high school years, he made his spending money fixing bicycles.

Educationally, Dennis didn't do well because he simply wasn't interested. Nobody would have guessed that either, since his father is a college professor and his mother is dean of women at the same school. They come from a long line of educators, but all that bookishness wasn't for Dennis.

> What kind of problem can you foresee in this situation where the parents value education and their son couldn't care less? Do you know any family with gaps like this? How do they handle them?

Today Dennis owns a bicycle shop. Bikes all over the place! New ones, used ones, broken-down bikes waiting for his expertise. No big deal? It is for Dennis. He lives in an area where bicycling is popular and the thing you may like about all this is what his mother and father said. While Dennis was still in high school, they told him, "Dennis, we'd really like you to graduate. But we're going to get off your back about grades and a good record and going to college. We're proud of the way you can do things we can't do. More than anything we want you to be you."

> Does your school emphasize individuality? Are your parents understanding? What are you doing to promote at home the attitude "I want you to be you"?

### HOW TO DISAGREE

"Never burn down your house to get rid of the mice." That's an old country proverb, but it's also wise advice. And its wisdom is as up-to-date as your next argument.

> How can we learn to disagree? At home? In the family?

As you read these "how to's" on disagreement, rate your family zero to ten (0–10). Zero for bad, ten for perfect.

*Rule 1:* Expect some disagreement. Don't be ashamed of anger. It's a natural part of being a thinking person. The only thing you need to regret is when you handle it badly.

*Rule 2:* Become skillful in the use of that simple little phrase, "I like you because...." Disagreement always goes better against a background loaded with praise.

*Rule 3:* Train yourself to say it softly. Letting it all hang out is important, but tone and volume can make a big difference. As the anger goes higher, lower your voice one octave instead of raising it two.

*Rule 4:* Keep your argument at home. It's a good idea when you're quarreling to commit yourself to the simple little adage "In public we will be 100 percent loyal to each other."

*Rule 5:* Recognize the fact that some disagreements can go unanswered and you can still love to the maximum. You don't have to like each other 100 percent to love 100 percent.

*Rule 6:* Get it out of your system quickly. Don't wait till next week. Of course, you may need to postpone it overnight, or at least a few hours. Sometimes it takes all the strength a person has just to go on breathing. But you had better get it out of your system before it gets buried inside you.

*Rule 7:* Keep these four words up front: "I'm sorry. I apologize."

Who started it, who did what to whom, is not as important as how can we get our relationship back together.

**In your family do you have some special techniques for disagreement which have been successful for you?**

END OF THE LINE FOR ERIC

**Is it ever right for a parent to say "You've had it. Don't come home any more until..."? What circumstances would justify this kind of drastic action? Does a parent "owe" everyone in the family a place to eat, sleep, to call home?**

Here is a letter from a father who is hurting:

Dear Dr. Shedd:

I have been forced to make a decision which I need to check with someone. Eric is eighteen. He's been into drugs, both heavy and light. He's been in trouble with the law often and has cost us more money than I can afford. I know that is the least important part of it, but I also know his brothers and sisters have had to do without a lot because of him. He constantly skips school, has dropped out two or three times, and he refuses to work.

Putting it all together, I finally asked myself some questions: Is it right for one child to destroy the atmosphere for everyone else in the home? When he has used up all his parents' reserves until they aren't good parents to the other children any more, is that right?

I've done everything I can think of to come up with some alternatives. I know I've been at fault, too. But I finally decided Eric had to go.

So I leveled with him. I tried to do it the best way I could. But I don't think there is any best way to do something like this. It was the hardest thing I ever did, but I told him, "Eric, you've had it. Whenever you will commit yourself to living by our rules; when you've proven long enough that you can straighten out your life, you're welcome back. Until then, you'll have to find some other place to live. I want you to know you're also on your own money-wise. Don't ask me for any more. I've exhausted my reserves for you and I'm not going to borrow to bail you out again. You can come visit us any time you're sober, any time you're willing to treat your Mom and me, your brothers and sisters like human beings. If you're going to destroy yourself, we're sorry. But we are not going to be destroyed with you. We will always love you, but we refuse to go down the tube with you."

> Back to the man's initial question,
> Is it right for a father to take a stand
> like that? How would you answer?

### ROSEMARY

Rosemary is one of those girls who makes you feel better for knowing her. She isn't a cheerleader or a class officer. Her grades are average. Yet Rosemary is somebody special and she is especially special to Keith.

Keith is her brother and he's in the eighth grade. Remember the eighth grade? You're too old to cry, but you shouldn't do anything drastic either, because you're not grown up enough to be completely on your own.

Now into the middle of Keith's eighth-grade dilemma, here comes Rosemary. Every Sunday afternoon Rosemary takes her brother out for a Coke. It's her idea. Of course, she says it's no big deal. But Keith thinks it is.

> Is there someone at your house
> who needs an ear? Maybe two ears,
> to surface what's going on inside?
> Would someone in your family be
> healthier if you really cared enough
> to get them aside regularly for the
> kind of therapy you could give
> them?

### WHAT ABOUT THOSE "BAD" THOUGHTS?

Letter from a high school student:

Dear Dr. Shedd:

Some of the things I think about girls really scare me. Know what I mean? All these good-looking girls in miniskirts. Even the cheerleaders drive me crazy. If you can go to hell for bad thoughts, then I'm on my way. You may think it's funny, but I don't. Some days I wonder if I have the dirtiest mind there ever was.

> Does he? Is he telling a truth? For boys only? Do girls have the same thoughts? Less? More? Did you get any help at your house on how to think straight about sex?

"Sex and Dating" was the title of a column I wrote regularly for *Teen Magazine*. Thousands of letters came from every state asking for straight talk on love, sex, dating, marriage. In seminars, conferences, retreats, bull sessions, and rallies, I talked with hundreds of teens. And every session I give them a chance to write questions. What do you think are the ten most asked questions on sex?

Here's the list:

1. How far can we go and still be safe?
2. Will masturbation hurt you?
3. Why should we wait till marriage?
4. How can I tell if I'm really in love?
5. How do you say no and still keep them liking you?
6. Is there any way to drop someone without hurting them?
7. Do normal people sometimes have feelings for members of their own sex? You know what I mean, like homosexuals and lesbians?
8. I have a friend who is pregnant. What should I tell her? (Often this means "I'm pregnant. What can I do?")
9. What about abortion?
10. When you get married, do you have to tell everything about what you have done?

Is your family the kind where you can share this list and discuss it? Do you have a brother, sister, or a friend who could use some help from you?

If you're asking some of these same questions, it might help to keep in mind you're not alone. I receive letters from thousands of teenagers across the nation who are struggling for answers to these questions.

### SAY IT BACK

These three little words could make all the difference to the people you live with: *say it back.*

Try it next time your sister is in a bad mood. Or when your mother is having one of her down days. The same goes for your father or your brother.

It goes like this. Your brother says, "Blah, blah, blah, you're always on the phone. Don't you know somebody else lives around here besides you?" Now, your first reaction is to blow right back, but in "say it back" you won't do that. Instead, you turn on some temporary calm and say, "I get your message. You think I talk too much."

BROTHER: "Yeah, Joe told me he tried for an hour to get me last night. It was really important."

Be steady now. Change the wording slightly and give it back like this: "Joe couldn't get you for an hour last night because I was on the phone? That's too bad. What happened to your deal?"

Now you have some possibility of unbraiding the knots between you. You keep saying it back until

1. He has it all out of his system.
2. You understand completely what's really bothering him.

3. He feels good, you feel good.
4. You've built a platform between you where you can meet again to settle future conflicts.

If you can learn this art, you will be a friend like very few friends. If you can develop it with skill at home this year, you will win friends and step up your happiness.

## SECTION II
### Would These Things Work in Your Family?

#### KEEP AMERICA CLEAN

Meet the Andersons. When I first saw them, they were walking in a ditch at the edge of town with sacks over their backs, carrying pointed sticks. There were the father, mother, and three children. I was heading for a speaking engagement one hundred miles south but, sensing a story, I stopped—and am I ever glad!

Once a month the Andersons dedicate a Saturday morning, seven o'clock until noon, to "keeping America clean." There is a section of road outside their town where people litter quite often. Beer cans, sandwich wrappers, bottles, brown-paper bags, Styrofoam cups, general debris from the nights before. And the Andersons do their part to pick up this litter.

How would any family get into this?

Bruce Anderson is a high school student. One evening he was riding with some of his friends. That's when Bruce, without thinking, threw a Coke can out the window. And wouldn't you know—just behind them was the highway patrol.

"See that sign, boy? Five hundred dollars for littering."

Fortunately, the justice of peace was an understanding person who liked young people. So instead of lowering the boom on Bruce's pocketbook, she gave him an alternative.

"You pick up a thousand cans along the road and I'll let you off. You have thirty days to get it done."

Bruce's father is one of those who would say, "Come on, I'll help you. We'll work it out together."

So they did. But by the time they had the first thousand cans, the whole family got involved. They decided together that this year they would give one Saturday each month to their own little "fight litter" project.

As I felt their enthusiasm, sensed their togetherness, I wondered: What would it do for our land if every family would spend one morning a month in beautifying the countryside with this kind of togetherness?

> Does your family have any kind of project you do together for other people? For the community? The nation? Could you?

### "NEVER DRIVE WHEN YOU'RE MAD"

Bob is sixteen, a new driver; and here's a story about him. His dad is a friend of mine and he was telling the story to a bunch of us over coffee. I think it deserves a larger audience.

"Sometimes I think we need to listen to our kids more. Let me tell you what happened last Sunday. We'd spent the afternoon at my sister's. As usual my brother-in-law and I got into an argument, and as usual, I went away mad.

"Well, all the way home in the car I was doing a slow burn. Running it over and over. Finally, Bob said, 'Dad, I want you to stop over at this drive-in. I'm thirsty.' He'd taken driver education and he really does handle the car well. So I let him have the wheel.

"But that isn't all he wanted. He also wanted the floor and he really put it to me. He gave me a big lecture on a film he'd seen in class. He said he had a pamphlet they have out on 'Never drive when you're mad.' I'll tell you for sure, he made me think."

> Anyone in your family drive like a madman? Any of your friends? Do you ever? Have you? Is this worth discussing at home?

## TEACHING KIDS SELF-LOVE

The Johnsons call it "I like me because" night and it sounds like a winner. Their idea is to keep everyone in the family involved in themselves.

Dear Dr. Shedd:

We want to tell you about a game we invented. We got the idea from a child psychologist we heard at a PTA meeting. She said: "Too many children grow up with a negative self-image, which sometimes comes from parents constantly correcting them, making them feel ashamed, putting on too much pressure for good behavior. By the time they get into the teen years, their pattern is so fixed that their low regard for their own worth can get them in trouble."

That may not be exactly the way she said it, but this is the way the whole thing came through to us. We were glad we heard her, because almost everybody needs affirmation and we sure do. So we agreed that once a week we would have "I like me because" night.

Each member of the family thinks up something good about himself to share with all of us. It doesn't have to be a big item, but sometimes it is. Everybody has a turn, including Mom and Dad. It may not sound like much, but we think in a world where there is so much put-down it's good to decide where we are up on ourselves.

Is this a possibility for your family? What three things do you like about you?

### "I MAKE A MOTION"

A smooth-running family I know operates on a deal which they call "the family council." This means any of the children or the parents have a place to be heard. Any motion, if it gets a second, is discussed. And sometimes the discussion goes on and on. Then when somebody calls for the question, they vote by ballot. Since there are secret ballots, nobody knows for sure who voted how. But when the votes are counted, they've all agreed, majority rules.

They even elected Dad head of the family. Twice someone moved for a new president, but both times they kept him on.

This family says this arrangement is very good for them. They vote on little things like "Where will we go out for dinner this week?" "What will we name the cat?" "Which movie will we choose?" They also vote on more important issues, like "We all agree Ted was wrong and what should we do about it?" "Dana thinks Mom and Dad aren't fair and she wants some place to be heard." "Dad has this nice job offer and he'd like to know what the family thinks."

Does this sound fair? It is. Plus, the father and mother say, "Sometimes when we have a difference of opinion we take it to the family and let them decide. We don't want our children to think everything is always cozy in a good relationship. Besides, we honestly believe that the total mind of our family in most things is better than one person deciding or two making the rules."

Sure would take a mature bunch to make this thing go, wouldn't it? But if you think those at your house would even be open to discussing it, it could be sensational:

for getting along;
for saying to each member of the family, "We respect
your opinion"; and
for understanding the weaknesses and the strong points
of democracy.

SECTION III
## Ways to Handle Your Parents*

Between parents and teenagers there are many potential
sore spots: money, music, clothes, cars, hair, homework,
friends, family (brothers, sisters, cousins, aunts, grandmas).
In fact, almost anything you mention could be a battle-
ground.

So, from what I've learned watching my own teenagers,
and from the ones I've seen who were getting the job done,
I've put together these "Twelve Rules for Handling Your
Parents." Why don't you go through them and then make
up your own?

1. *Remember, you're no bargain to live with either!*
If there is one thing as tough as being a teenager, it's
having one. So when things get rough between you and
your folks, suppose you go straight down the hall and look
in the mirror. You'll do a great thing for your future if you
learn to start analyzing your people-conflicts with the question "Where am I wrong?"

2. *Remember, nobody gets everything he wants. There
are other people in the world besides you!*
You're at the age when you begin wanting more. You
want to try some new ideas, to feel more grown-up, to impress more people. But perhaps you had better back off

* This section is adapted from Dr. Charlie Shedd's book, *The Stork Is
Dead* (Waco, Texas: Word Publishing Co., 1968), p. 85.

now and then to see the whole picture at your house and in the world. I hope you get some of the things you want, things that will make you happy, but don't forget the others —including your mom and dad. They like and want nice things, too.

3. *Let others have their way sometimes, especially with the little things.*

The wise teenager doesn't try to win every argument. There are dozens of small deals where it really doesn't matter who comes out on top. If you show your parents you are willing to give in a lot of the time, you're being smart. They are more likely to cooperate when it's some big deal you've just got to have. It is hard to turn down a teenager today who said yesterday, "I think you're right, Dad. I hadn't thought of it like that." Learning to live with this kind of give-and-take is great for another reason. It is excellent preparation for life on your own.

4. *Show a little sympathy.*

Trying to be "understanding" 100 percent of the time is a good start for bettering any relationship. What it means is that you try to see things through the other person's eyes.

If you would make the effort, you might find out some things about your folks. During your teen years it's possible your dad is having his toughest time ever. He may be readjusting his thinking about how great he is. He's pulling down some of his goals. Perhaps he's battling to keep his spirits up.

Your mother may be approaching the time of life which isn't easy for women. All kinds of fears and odd sensations go through some minds at middle age. Try really caring about how they feel.

We have this one character at our house who can get just about anything he wants. You know how he does it?

When he comes home from school, he puts his arm around his mom and says, "How'd it go today?" At night sometimes he sits by his dad and says, "You look tired, Pop! Have a hard day?" He really does care. "All God's children have trouble these days"—that means your mom and dad. too.

5. *Make a solemn vow: "I will say thank you to each of my folks at least once every day."*

Saying thanks to your parents is an important key to building respect for one another. It will give you a sense of pride by making them feel good and will help them feel appreciated for their sincere efforts to be good parents.

6. *At least once a week do something nice for your parents.*

It doesn't need to be something like buying a new car or paying off the mortgage. Any little thing will do so long as (a) they weren't expecting it, and (b) you get the message across that you'd like to make life a little easier for them. I know one girl who, during her teenage years, would say to her parents now and then, "This Friday I'm going to stay home and babysit. You're going out and have a good time." What do you suppose that did for their feelings toward her?

7. *Learn to say "I'm sorry."*

Nothing marks you as a person of character than this. Discharging the obligation of your errors with an apology is a mature way of handling yourself. Of course you will make a mistake once in a while. We all do. And other people will be more prepared to make amends when *they* should if you do it when *you* should. Few things can lift the level of human relations like honest humility properly expressed.

8. *Never do anything to betray their trust or make them question your honesty.*

The first time you lie to your parents, you have put your foot on a treacherous road. It may be difficult to appreciate this till you are a parent, but it is great to always know that your children will tell you the truth. You can imagine how much easier it is to say yes to someone like this. When your folks lose faith in you and it's your fault, you have lost more than you want to lose.

9. *To eliminate some arguments, work up a few agreements in advance.*

The use of the telephone, for instance. Be reasonable; your parents have friends, too. Ahead of time, you can settle some questions like How often can you date? Whom can you date? Where can you go? What time will you be in? How much allowance will you get? What work will you do around the house? How much privacy will they give you? How much will you give them in return? Dozens of these things can be settled by prearrangement, rather than fought over later. Smart teenagers think ahead!

10. *Ask their advice now and then on something big enough to make them feel important.*

There isn't a parent alive who wouldn't react favorably to the four words "I need your help." Parents really do know some things worth knowing. They would be flattered. And would that ever improve the atmosphere around home!

11. *Tell them you'd like to know about sex straight from them.*

So, they were brought up in a day when things were different. But they must know a little. I honestly believe a lot of parents would like to try. If you'd only prompt them a little, or show some open-mindedness long enough, or keep a straight face long enough, maybe they wouldn't be half bad. And the way I'd begin would be something like this: "I know you're a lot smarter than some of the people who have been telling me about sex. Will you answer some questions for me?"

12. *Learn to communicate!*
Communication is one of the most needed and important parts of any relationship. Just as learning to accept and adjust to your friends, the same is true about your parents. You need to accept them and make adjustments for your differences. This probably won't happen without some honest and open communication. Don't be afraid to open your mouth!

*Empathy* is one of the most beautiful words in the English language. Empathy means: "Capacity for participating in another's feelings"; "Imaginative identification of oneself with another person"; "Entering fully through imagination into another's feelings or motives."

Parents, brothers, sisters, aunts, uncles, cousins, neighbors, the man who pumps your gas, the lady checking your groceries, that crabby teacher, John, Sally, Peter, Mary Ann —every person you know is asking: "Does anybody out there care about me?"

If you can get yourself out of the way long enough to develop true empathy, you've done a great thing.

You've done a great thing for you.

For your family.

For the whole world.

# IRENE KASSORLA

**Dr.** Irene Kassorla's revolutionary new approach to mental illness has earned her international fame as an expert in schizophrenia, autism, and family therapy. While still an undergraduate at UCLA (where she earned her B.A. and M.A. degrees in psychology) she was responsible for designing a new method for treating mentally disturbed children. Soon afterward, she traveled the world helping mute psychotic patients to speak. In 1966 she was invited to England to duplicate her work and conduct more research. She remained in Britain three years and earned her Ph.D. from the University of London.

She is also famous as a television personality: Dr. Kassorla's group therapy sessions can be seen on television all over the United States. Presently she lives in Los Angeles, where she is well known for her lectures and internationally best-selling book, *Putting It All Together.*

# *You and the Person You May Marry*

"How do I know if I'm really in love?"

"What is love all about?"

"Could this be love?"

Love is probably one of life's most inspiring subjects. Also one of the most exciting and bewildering. But examining what the wise have said about love may only add to our dilemma.

Shakespeare wrote, "Love is a devil deserving a whip."

Longfellow quipped, "Love keeps out cold better than a cloak."

Emerson said, "Love is the essence of God."

Your personal reaction to love may involve conflicting feelings. For you, it may be passionate bliss or agonized panic. It could be compulsive overeating or inability to eat one thing. You might experience increased pulse rate at one moment, numbness the next. Suddenly, you're marveling at your insight, then all at once you feel blurry. Next, a feeling of love for all mankind may overcome you, and that may be followed by irrational suspicion. One minute you find yourself hyperactive, the next you'll be relaxed, drowsy.

If all these divergent feelings leave you jumbled, don't worry. This is normal. And part of the confusion comes from the mix-up between our concepts of romantic love and our need for mature love.

Romantic love is a magical experience of heightened euphoria enjoyed particularly at the beginning stages of a relationship. During these early days of dating many people lose their judgment. They call their romantic emotions *ecstasy* (from the Greek word *ekstasis*, which means "being beside oneself, deranged, beyond all reason or self-control").

Romance is often based on ecstatic nonlogic. Whether it's the frenzied joy of elation, or the miserable discomfort of anxiety, romance is a complicated mixture of pleasure and pain. But that isn't all. Each of these feelings can be enjoyed or suffered on many occasions. French writer Marcel Proust thought romance had little to do with reality and was an occupation of the idle that was full of anguish. Proust considered the romantic condition an illusion, where we blindly give our loves remarkable characteristics and qualities we *wish* them to have, quite unrelated to facts or their actual personalities.

It is possible to give the person we love some qualities they do not really have.

Sometimes this exaggerating goes on so long that the lover is blinded to all truth. In other relationships such fantasizing may be short-term.

Wise couples use their dating experience to learn more about each other. As their illusions dim, and their sight improves, they do not panic. They can face the facts, because they are also discovering many good things about each other which didn't show up in the early romance.

Mature love has a chance for survival. When two people can join lives and still maintain their individuality, dignity and integrity, love can develop. Mature love is based on mutual respect, companionability, and rapport. There's a sense of fulfillment when the two are together, with genuine care and concern for the other. Here's a famous psychiatrist's poignant description of love, that sums up these feelings:

"When the satisfaction or security of another person becomes as significant to one as is one's own satisfaction and security, then the state of love exists."

*Harry Stack Sullivan.*

## Evaluating the Prospects

Songwriters say, "First comes love, then comes marriage."

But *living happily ever after* isn't an automatic by-product of the wedding ceremony. As the writer of this chapter, I want you to know my position. I believe that marriage is the healthiest way to live and can be an ideal human state. However, I also know this requires hard work, commitment, and dedication to mature love.

One of the first things to evaluate is *compatibility*. Compatibility means there will be similarities in many areas—religion, race, education, family background, early childhood experiences, cultural opportunities, and others. For example, if you were raised on a farm and your intended grew up in a major metropolis, you would be *low* on compatibility in that area.

Compatibility can also include preferences in food, music, entertainment, and even your choices for television viewing. Couples are most compatible when they share similar objectives in choosing friends, clothing, pets, and living style (suburbia vs. the city, houses vs. apartments, and so forth). Differences in tastes, manners, travel experience, prejudices, and political background are also important issues.

Even the education, place of birth, age and income of parents can affect compatibility. Researchers suggest the higher the compatibility, the lower the rate of problems and eventual divorce. Experts on divorce say that couples who are most compatible during dating find it easiest to keep their relationships healthy and meaningful once married.

Opposite view from a high school student:

"I don't think the area in which you live (religion or some of the other things) matters that much. You have to have something in common, but it's neat when some things aren't. The things you don't have in common you can adjust to and learn about. A perfect love and marrage isn't just a matched couple. It's a learning experience."

When the prospects for marriage are good, both partners actively maintain a caring relationship. Each looks forward to the other's company. Both partners expend great effort to keep the relationship alive and happy. There is a feeling of cohesion with enthusiastic plans for tomorrow and constant referrals to "our," "us," "we."

## Disagreement

You're on the right track if you can accept the possibility of times when you'll actually dislike (maybe even hate) each other. Don't worry. This is not unusual. It means your communication has bogged down temporarily. At these times each person needs to work at *stopping* the blaming and *starting* to share more feelings.

A person who is a "good bet" for marriage doesn't hold grudges when a fight is over. Instead, each looks at his or her own part in creating the misunderstanding, and is willing to assume responsibility for it. It is essential now for each to listen to all complaints. This is the time to share information, to practice communication skills, and to bring feelings to the surface.

## Change

The ability to adapt and change long-cherished points of view will be tested. Each partner will be challenged to limit well-established personal bias and modify different values.

Healthy partners are sensitive to changing moods. They aspire to maintain a loving level of respect for new ideas. They meet these new opinions with kindness. These qualities of flexibility can prove to be a major determining factor in the longevity of a future marriage.

## Bad Bets for Marriage

What are some of the "caution" signs?

Couples immersed in the passion of a romantic moment may ignore the gnawing uncertainties that could trouble them later. Each is afraid to lose his or her lover. Then the rationalizations take over and cover up the doubts.

"Everything will be fine once we're married" could be foolish thinking. Problems should be dealt with at the time they occur, openly and honestly. Mutually comfortable, practical solutions need to be reached. Problems left to fester may prove cancerous and incurable in marriage. It's far easier and less expensive to break an engagement than a marriage.

You may find your own experience in the following list:

Danger signs:
• pressure applied by the other
• dissatisfaction with the other's expression of affection
• strong parental disapproval
• constant quarreling and bickering
• recurrent doubts

- desire to make changes in the partner's personality
- disapproval of partner's friends
- a relationship which operates in only one area
- a wish to alter the ambitions, dreams, goals of the partner
- feelings of regret regarding the engagement
- repeated episodes of "breaking the engagement"
- either partner's excessively close attachment to parents
- considering demands of the partner unfair or irrational

Did the above list ring any bells with you? Which of these have you felt in a relationship?

One teenager with a positive parental relationship took this list to the dinner table and had a lively discussion with his mother, father, and older sister. Good idea for you?

Can you add other warning signs out of your own experience or the experience of friends?

## Dating

Researchers note there are few divorces among people who marry after twenty-eight. This is probably due to the increased information they have gathered during their teens and twenties.

Falling in and out of love is a healthy adolescent activity. Dating allows the valuable experience of interacting with many different personalities. This is vital preparation for making a wise choice in marriage.

So, if you are not yet into a permanent commitment, you

can be glad for one thing: you have plenty of opportunity to learn about yourself and take time to ask questions.

"What can I expect from this relationship?"

"Is this what it feels like to be an adult?"

"How much can I let myself go now? Later?"

Going steady offers an intensified period for evaluating feelings of being committed to one person. This can be a crucial time for making final judgment. "Would it be prudent for us to proceed with marriage plans?" Going steady also provides opportunity to sample the kind of cooperation and compromise that marriage will require.

With sufficient preview, couples can be more confident about their decision to move on to the next step. Only adequate timing can make the engagement announcements (and the wedding plans) what they should be for everyone.

## Honesty in Long-Range Planning

Can you be truthful when you're in love? Have you been worried that honestly expressing your love feelings will be dangerous? Are you afraid you'll be rejected if you dare to be vulnerable and express yourself openly?

One of my young patients related her conflicts like this:

"Whenever I'm honest with guys, they disappear. When I show I like them, it's like the 'kiss of death.' But everytime I'm stand-offish, act critical, and practically ignore them, they come grabbing and clutching at me. Admitting I'm crazy in love seems to kill everything. So I just lie and pretend like I don't care about them."

Sidestepping the truth may be one of the worst of all games. Most of us are familiar with game playing. But hiding our feelings and appearing bored may be asking for big trouble. A long-term relationship with someone unable to handle getting close can lead to disaster. If a prospective lover is excited by you only when you're pretending to be disinterested, you're opting for loneliness in a self-made prison. What if you end up with a partner who is so frightened by intimacy, so afraid of affection, that he or she will unconsiously welcome criticism and abuse?

It is far healthier to be loving, vulnerable, and open. Take your chances. Express yourself truthfully and state your feelings. You may discover that your honesty will turn off some. You may frighten those who are unable to deal with your warmth and they may leave you. But you need only one person to stay who can be honest and genuine.

There are people who are able to handle honesty, and you won't find them playing hard-to-get. In psychological terms, "like attracts like." That is, someone who plays games will attract another game-player. When you are authentic, you'll be able to find someone who is your equal. Then your self-worth and self-esteem can flourish with an honest, loving person at your side. You're on your way to a solid and loving person.

## Secrets to Getting Along, Close-up

This section is designed to offer new patterns for interacting. It is to help you avoid irksome disputes and tedious squabbles. Here are some guidelines for getting along better, close-up.

Every successful association needs well-defined, mutually acceptable rules. Roles must be assigned, jobs delegated, expectations clarified.

Here are some typical areas where rules spelled out can avert future problems:

• financing (who pays bills, budgeting, "our" money vs. "my" money, and the like)

• friends (yours, mine, both, neither)

• privacy and separate territory (space, vacations, spare time)

- sexuality (frequency, loyalty, commitment, intimacy, affection)
  - manners
  - values, fighting, morality
  - future aspirations, goals
  - children (if any, number, child-rearing philosophy)

It works best when ideas and suggestions are aired, and rules discussed, *before* marriage.

It's naive and painful to wait until the troubles start. Setting rules down early in the relationship will ward off partners feeling abused or misunderstood later.

> **Rules to avert future problems can be a big help.**
>
> **From the list above, select those most important to you.**
>
> **When do you think rules like these should be discussed?**

## Positives

Many couples complain that their partners rarely compliment them. In some of these relationships each is able to rave about the other to a friend, but for some reason neither can praise his or her mate face to face.

Healthy people thrive on positive input. Human behavior research suggests that behavior rewarded and reinforced tends to multiply.

Here is one example of do's and don'ts:

| DO | DON'T |
|---|---|
| "I really like your hair. You look great!" | "It's about time you made a change. You finally look good." |

We're all like small children, aching for approval from the people we value. It feels good to know we're admired. Go tell your love he or she is important to you. Be positive. Do it now.

## Talk-It-Out Sessions

Ideally, couples express their feelings the moment a controversy or uncomfortable situation arises. But this may be rare, as most people have difficulty sharing their emotions on the spot. Yet feelings which do not surface may be acted out with a long list of destructive "insteads."

- overeating
- alcoholism
- drug addiction
- overworking
- oversleeping
- inertia
- jealousy
- extra-marital behavior
- psychosomatic illnesses: headaches, acne, colds, colitis, asthma, piles, ulcers, and a host of others

All of these are costly alternatives to honesty, to the expression of feelings, to talk.

For some couples, having a regular time to discuss problems will be a good thing. At these times they can discuss feelings, air differences, share hurts, talk over disappointments, bring up resentments. During these sessions each partner will have a turn at ventilating and, above all, listening.

## Decision Making

Distressed couples sometimes employ unhealthy *role-playing* in making decisions. What does this mean? It means that one partner assumes the role of the parent, and makes decisions independent of the mate. The left-out partner might feel ignored, resentful. So there is the possibility of an unconscious striking back (to balance the ledger) by being critical, sarcastic, impossible to satisfy. In such a relationship the fun stops while bickering, pouting, and long periods of uncomfortable silence take over.

Example:

Friends call and invite a married couple to dinner. The person answering the phone could say:

| THIS: | or THIS: |
|---|---|
| "Your invitation sounds wonderful. I'd love to come. I'll check with my husband [wife]. Can I call you back?" | "I'd love to come. We'll definitely be there. See you Saturday night at eight." |

Unless it's an emergency, decisions which involve both people should be okayed by both. Each partner will be consulted before the decision is made.

Here, the partner who accepted the invitation without consulting took on the role of the parent/authority. The other became the child who could get even by sabotaging the fun of the evening or "getting back" later.

## Compromise

One of the most fundamental concepts that can predict the success or failure of a marriage is willingness to compromise. Compromising skills may take years to learn, but in a marriage, you'll have a lifetime to practice.

Compromising works something like this:

A couple agrees they need a second automobile. One partner is convinced that life will not be endurable unless they purchase an exciting $10,000 sportscar. The other, more conservative ("Don't be ridiculous. You're insane. How extravagant can you get?"), argues that a $1,000 used car will do.

Any position of compromise would suggest settling these differences somewhere down the middle. In this case, they might buy a new car for $5,000. Then one partner would have far less than originally fantasized. But the other would be spending much more than he or she first thought sensible.

Another essential for compromise: Each partner must be a good sport. This requires that each explore the positive aspects of their compromised position. In the event the compromise proves to be unsatisfactory, there will be no complaints. No "I told you so." No regrets. Compromising offers a vehicle to settle differences and get on with the happy business of loving.

One of the most common areas of compromise is who does what in the kitchen. Many new couples have to learn to disregard parental roles (woman cooks and cleans) and find their own solution. If the man likes to cook, he should; the woman can then do the dishes. Or vice-versa. Whatever the arrangement, sharing of duties is best when a compromise is struck and kept.

## Alternative Life Styles

Working on various continents has allowed me an extraordinary view of marriage. My observations of families in other countries clearly show that they have problems too.

No matter where they live, few couples find it easy to establish and maintain an intimate relationship. It seems that all people everywhere experience difficulty staying in love.

In all relationships there is a common phenomenon I call "distance." By distance, I mean that people feel uncomfortable and anxious when they get too close. So they develop ways to separate and stay apart. There is a terror (sometimes unconscious) of being totally dependent on one other person.

We know we're mortal, and the precious love we cherish could die. Thinking about the prospect of grieving and feeling helpless is overwhelming. If we're not worrying about death, we're suffering from fantasies of being rejected. Due to these deeply embedded fears, few of us dare to love deeply. We rationalize, "If I don't get too loving, too close, I won't get hurt."

Many couples looking for alternatives to marriage are unwittingly creating emotional distance to reduce their fears. Their underlying psychological motivation is to create distance.

A sizable number of couples today, although a minority, are investigating alternative life styles. It is important for us to look at some of these alternate modes.

## Co-Marital and Open Relationships

In a co-marital relationship, couples regularly exchange partners with the consent of their spouses. Co-marital sex is distinguished from extra-marital sex as being open and shared, rather than covert and secretive. In these cases, the couples might make a contract or come to some kind of prior agreement. Additional members are brought into the marriage to play a role in the activities and planning of the now expanded family.

This is a voluntary family group of three or more adults. Each is committed to maintain the relationship in a manner regarded as "married," and it is most commonly called "group marriage." These members usually develop structures for sharing personal resources.

Open marriage has some similarities to co-marital relationships. The major exception here is that extra partners do not join the family constellation.

One focus of these alternatives is the search for personal identity, flexibility, equality, privacy, honesty. Proponents of these life styles feel traditional marriage prohibits these goals.

These styles of living ignore the reality of how people group up: their deeply embedded early conditioning; their need for dependency; feeling secure, wanted. It can be extremely painful knowing someone you love is out for the night, copulating with another partner. It would also be difficult for someone with a sense of self to allow his or her partner the freedom of open companionship.

## Extra-Marital Behavior

As an experienced counselor, I call these substitutes "insteads." I believe that much extra-marital behavior has little to do with sex. Rather, it is an "instead" for anger. And much of the work of marriage counselors is helping couples with communication problems to express their anger. Psychologists and psychiatrists believe this is true: Getting anger directly out-of-the-mouth, targeted to the person involved, is usually difficult. Few of us have the learned skills, so we use "insteads" (substitutes).

This is why I believe most of these alternative life styles are smokescreens hiding blocked feelings and limiting real communication. The alternatives chosen are "insteads" for expressing anger, disappointment, and frustration. They prohibit dealing with important feelings of inadequacy, fear of abandonment, and getting close. I suspect that many of these alternative-life-style partners engage in sex outside the marriage without the permission or knowledge of their spouse.

In all these varied alternative life styles, too much energy may be put into outside relationships. This enormous expenditure of emotions (plus planning and time required) is costly. Personal development and effectiveness suffer. Too much of the focus centers away from the marriage. Intimacy vanishes and each partner is made less valuable by the increased availability of others.

## Maleness and Femaleness

Popular magazines are jamming the newsstands today with nude pictures of the body beautiful. While buying groceries, shoppers are titillated with shelves of periodicals showing living proof of the physical differences between men and women.

If you were a biologist, you would use the term *phenotypic*. This is the word for visual characteristics of an organism. The word means: "Men and women are different physically," phenotypically different. But if you were a psychologist or psychiatrist, you could also take an opposite view. You could point to many basic similarities among men and women. You could see clearly how much alike they are emotionally.

We all need security, acceptance, the safety of belonging. We are also similar in our fears of being rejected, aging, death. We all need respect too in the way we worry about measuring up to society's opinion of what it means to be male or female.

## Macho

Unrealistic models for maleness and femaleness are nothing new. They date back to the ancient Greeks and the Romans, and before. To be male long ago often meant absolute authority. A man had to be strong, dauntless, a patriarch protecting his family against all invaders. Women weren't important; they bore children, they were servants, companions for their husbands. That, at least, was the stereotype.

More recently, the roles of male and female in our society has sometimes been defined by the "macho" theory. According to macho dogma, a real man is fearless, rugged, close-mouthed, unsentimental. He never cries, looks frightened, or shows emotion. He's competitive, aggressive, and an avid sports fan. His lustful sexual prowess is believed to be constant. So are his virility and strength. This is obviously a mythical creature.

The macho reality of femininity is equally absurd. This nonsensical idea suggests that the female is weak and unsophisticated. She will be nonsensual, nonsexual, and bored during intercourse (which she only tolerates for the sake of her husband). She has no interest in continued education, personal growth, or a career. She is her mate's slave, housekeeper, bearer of his children. She always considers him before herself.

While this absence of self-esteem and personal dignity may sound ridiculous, some people enter marriage saddled with these ego-damaging myths. Almost always the result will be feelings of inadequacy and unfulfillment. Every couple getting married (or already married) is wise to disregard these stereotyped concepts and develop their own personal concepts. Role models change through the centuries, and even within decades. The "macho" ideal is as outdated as the knight in shining armor rescuing his damsel in distress.

> What is your description of a healthy male?
>
> _____
>
> What is your description of a healthy female?
>
> _____

Many women today are looking forward to homemaking and mothering. That is fine for them. But an ever-increasing number of women enter higher education and careers. These women feel it's possible to combine family life with work outside the home. That's fine, too.

In a good marriage, *both* partners take turns experiencing various rols. Both can be agressive, noncompetitive, strong, weak, protector, protected, wage-earner, parent. In mature relationships, each partner is given the freedom to experiment, to trade roles.

## Marital Sex

Sexual intercourse is an extension of the caring and sharing bond couples enjoy when they're married. It's another way to experience intimacy and love in a meaningful relationship.

It is important in good marital sex for *both* partners to enjoy themselves. The focus should be on *mutual* pleasure, *mutual* satisfaction, *mutual* fun. It's good to remember that sexual adjustment takes time. It takes time to learn more about your mate and to acquire expertise in lovemaking. In fact, great sex could be "a twenty-year warm-up."

As time passes, each partner discovers his or her own sensuality. Each learns preferences, understands individual passions, appreciates secret desires.

## The Word Is "Both"

In a good relationship, the responsibility of enjoyable sex is assumed by both husband and wife. Success depends on both partners' willingness to develop necessary skills, timing, techniques. Neither is responsible for initiating sex or being assertive. Healthy lovers are equally aggressive, equally interested, equally enthusiastic.

## Common Deterrents

Couples who experience sexual difficulties can usually work problems out together. In some cases, professional help will be advantageous. For most "young marrieds," education is an important first step.

There is too little sex education in most of our backgrounds. Few parents offer their children help in this area. Rather, the dialogue is "Don't look, don't touch, don't feel." Passion is taboo . . . so are discussions about sex. But husband and wife can seek out information they missed as children. They can educate themselves in biological, physical, psychological data. Dr. Eleanor Hamilton, an expert on sexual problems, lists barriers which may act as deterrents to satisfactory sex. She says those barriers are:

1. Ignorance of basic psychological and biological facts.

2. Clumsiness and lack of sensitivity in the performance or the love ritual.

3. Fear of asking for the satisfaction of a felt need.

4. Muscular tenseness, derived from original protection from emotions.

5. Inability to concentrate upon lovemaking without the interference of other concerns.

6. Feeling of shame.

7. Fear of pregnancy.

Being able to communicate fears, yearnings and reactions to each other is important, along with accepting the other's sexual longings, fantasies, and differences. When both partners are flexible, there's fun with the unexpected, unplanned sexual moments, and a playful search for innovation.

Sex, in a literal sense, is a beautiful way to erase distance. When two bodies interlock in loving union, an exquisite physical bonding seals the emotions. In marital sex, feelings of tenderness and safety encircle the experience. Being together in each other's arms is a comfortable sweetness which often cradles the couple to sleep. This is our bed, our marriage, our love.

Marital sex is the expression of loving another, and enjoying the beauty and perfection of two healthy, sensual selves. Sex at its best should be a precious way to get close to you and the person you marry.

# JIM DOBSON

Dr. James C. Dobson is Associate Clinical Professor of Pediatrics, University of Southern California School of Medicine, and author of three best-selling books, *Dare to Discipline*, *Hide or Seek*, and *What Wives Wish Their Husbands Knew about Women*. He has appeared on several national talk shows and has spoken for fifteen years on the subject of family relationships. His impact has been felt by thousands as he speaks openly and frankly about discipline in the home and offers practical advice to parents on child rearing.

# *You and Your Own Parenting*

A woman with seven rambunctious children boarded a Los Angeles bus and sat in the seat behind me. Her hair was a mess and the black circles under her eyes revealed a state of utter exhaustion. As she stumbled past me with her wiggling tribe, I asked, "Do all those children belong to you, or is this some kind of picnic?"

She looked at me through half-squinted eyes and said, "They're all mine, and believe me, it's *no* picnie!"

Small children have an uncanny ability to unravel the adult nervous system. They are noisy and they make incredible messes and they bicker with one another and their noses drip and they scratch the furniture and they have more energy in their fat little fingers than Mama has in her entire weary body.

How well I remember the day my wife put our four-month-old son, Ryan, on the dressing table to change his diapers. As soon as she removed his wet garments, he made like a fountain and sprayed the wall and the carpet and a picture of Boy Blue. She had no sooner repaired the damage than the telephone rang. While she was gone, Ryan was struck by a sudden attack of projectile diarrhea, and he machine-gunned his crib and the rest of the nursery. By the time my patient wife bathed her son and scoured the room, she was near exhaustion. She dressed Ryan in clean, sweet-smelling clothes and put him over her shoulder affectionately. At that moment he deposited his breakfast down her neck and into her undergarments. That evening, I found her sitting in a darkened corner of the family room, muttering quietly to herself and slowly shaking her head from side to side.

For discussion and personal musing:
"We know that every child is an individual and that he travels at his own tailor-made time schedule... if he is at all normal, as he probably is, then you will have the reassurance that he is steadily (though not evenly) moving forward to higher levels of maturity. This reassurance will place you in a better position ...you will always be confronted by a phase of time! The total ground plan is beyond your control. It is too complex and mysterious to be altogether entrusted to human hands. So, nature takes over most of the task, and simply invites your assistance."

## Children Are Expensive

There's no doubt about it: children are expensive little people. To raise them properly will require the very best that you can give of your time, effort, and financial resources. However, to those who have never experienced parenthood, the job may appear ridiculously simple. Such people remind me of a person watching the game of golf for the first time, thinking "That looks easy. All you have to do is hit that little white ball out there in the direction of the flag." The duffer then steps up to the tee, draws back the club, and dribbles the "little white ball" about nine feet to the left. Accordingly, if you have criticized your own mother and father for their obvious mistakes and failures, the game of raising kids is more difficult than it looks!

So the responsibilities of parenthood are costly and complex. Am I suggesting, then, that married couples should remain childless? Certainly not! The family that loves children and wants to experience the thrill of procreation should not be frightened by the challenge of parenthood.

Speaking from my own perspective as a father, there has been no greater moment in my life than when I gazed into the eyes of my infant daughter and, five years later, those of my son. What could be more exciting than seeing those tiny human beings begin to blossom and grow and learn and love? And what reward could be more meaningful than having my little boy or girl climb into my lap as I sit by the fire, hugging my neck and whispering, "I love you, Dad." Oh yes, children are expensive, but they're worth the price.

## You as a Parent

Assuming that you want to become a parent, what kind of mother or father will you be? Will you have a "game plan" or will you muddle through by random trial and error?

Perhaps you will be like a friend of mine who flew his single-engine airplane toward a small country airport. He arrived as the sun had dropped behind a mountain at the close of the day, and by the time he maneuvered into a position to land, he could not see the hazy field below. He had no lights on his plane and there was no one on duty at the airport. He circled the runway for another attempt to land, but the darkness had then become even more impenetrable. For two hours he flew his plane around and around in the blackness of the night, knowing that he faced certain death when his fuel was expended. Then, as greater panic gripped him, a miracle occurred. Someone on the ground heard the continuing drone of his engine and realized his predicament. That merciful man drove his car back and forth on the runway to show my friend the location of the airstrip, and then let his lights cast their beam from the far end while he landed.

I think of that story whenever I am coming down at night in a commercial airliner. As I look ahead, I can see the green lights bordering the runway which tell the captain where to direct the plane. If it stays between those lighted boundaries, all will be well. There is safety in that illuminated zone, but disaster lies to the left or right.

As new parents, there should be clearly marked boundaries telling us where to steer the family ship. We require some guiding *principles* which will help us raise our children in safety and health. Listed below are some principles which will serve as beacons to mark the safety zone in raising children.

## The First Beacon:
### LET LOVE BE YOUR GUIDE

The cornerstone for all human relationships is love. All of us require it, but children are especially dependent on human affection. It has been known for several decades that an infant who is not loved—not touched and caressed—will often die of a strange deterioration called marasmus.

As early as the thirteenth century, Frederick II conducted an experiment with fifty infants. He wanted to see what language the children would speak if they never had the opportunity to hear the spoken word. To accomplish this dubious research project, he assigned foster mothers to bathe and nurse the children but forbade them to fondle, pet, or talk to their charges. The experiment failed because all fifty infants died.

Hundreds of more recent studies indicate that the mother-child relationship during the first year of life is apparently vital to the infant's survival. The father-child relationship is also of great significance to healthy development. Accordingly, an unloved child is truly the saddest phenomenon in all nature.

But why should parents have to be reminded of the need to love their children? Isn't that an automatic response for a sensitive mother or father? Yes, children are easy to love—unless we are so busy that we seldom give them a thought. The greatest threat to meaningful family life is not deliberate hostility or rejection; it is a product of time pressure and overextended schedules and physical exhaustion. We Americans are often in such a ridiculous hurry to get where we're going that we huff and puff our lives away. There was a time when a man didn't fret if he missed a stagecoach; he'd just catch another one next month. Now if a fellow misses a section of a revolving door he's thrown into despair.

## Thirty-seven Seconds

A team of researchers recently wanted to learn how much time per day middle-class fathers spend with their small children. First they asked a group of fathers to estimate the time spent with their one-year-old youngsters each day; they received an average reply of fifteen to twenty minutes. To verify these claims, the investigators attached microphones to the shirts of the small children for the purpose of recording actual verbalizations. The results of this study are shocking: the average time spent by these middle-class fathers with their children was thirty-seven seconds per day! Their direct interaction was limited to 2.7 encounters daily, lasting ten to fifteen seconds each! That represents the contribution of fatherhood for millions of America's children.

Who is the inevitable loser from this breathless life style? It's the little guy or gal you see leaning against the wall, hands in the pockets of his or her blue jeans. They miss their fathers during the long day and tag around after them at night, saying, "Play ball, Dad?" But Dad has a briefcase full of work to be done. Mom had promised to take them to the park this afternoon but she had to go to that Women's Auxiliary meeting at the last minute. The kids get the message—their folks are busy again. So they drift into the family room and watch two hours of cartoons and reruns on television.

Children don't fit onto a "to do" list very well. It takes time to introduce them to good books—it takes time to listen, once more, to the skinned-knee episode and talk about the bird with the broken wing. Yet these are the building blocks of self-esteem, held together with the mortar of love. They seldom materialize amid busy timetables. Instead, crowded lives produce fatigue—and fatigue produces irritability—and irritability produces indifference—and indifference can be interpreted by the child as a lack of genuine affection and personal worth.

## Prison Experiment

Children who have been ignored or neglected are likely to carry their emotional scars into adult life. This fact was illustrated again in a recent conversation with a research psychologist who visited my office. He had been studying the early childhoods of inmates at a state prison in Arizona. He and his associates were seeking common characteristics which the prisoners shared, hoping to unlock the causes for their antisocial behavior.

It was initially assumed that poverty would be the common thread, but the findings contradicted this expectation. The inmates came from all socioeconomic levels of society, though most of them attempted to excuse their crimes by professing to have been poor. Instead, the researchers discovered one fundamental characteristic shared by the prisoners: *an absence of adult contact in their early home lives.* As children, they spent most of their time in the company of their peers . . . or altogether alone. The conclusion is inescapable: there is no substitute for loving parental leadership in the early development of children.

Let me offer a word of advice to new families—keep the pace of living under control. Don't let your desire for cars and houses and furniture lead you to moonlight when you ought to be taking walks and singing songs and examining pretty leaves and caterpillars with your children. They will grow up so quickly, and your opportunity to build a foundation of love is a fleeting responsibility.

## The Second Beacon:
### DARE TO DISCIPLINE

In 1970, I wrote a book for parents and teachers entitled *Dare to Discipline*. As the name implies, I urged adults to have the courage to give their children the discipline they require for healthy growth and development. I still believe this to be true, but there are two costly errors to be avoided in this important aspect of parent-child relationships.

### TOO HARD

The first mistake commonly made in disciplining children is a tendency to be too harsh and oppressive. A parent can destroy a child through mean, whimsical, unloving punishment. And unfortunately, many children suffer parental wrath on a regular basis. One study recently showed that more children under five years of age are killed by their parents each year than die of disease! As many as 60,000 children are beaten to death annually in America.

Of course, there are firm laws designed to protect children from cruel punishment. However, it is almost impossible to shield a youngster from mental and emotional torture if the parents stay within certain limits. I counseled one unfortunate teenager whose brutal father had beaten her throughout childhood. On one occasion after she accidentally wet her bed during the night, he wrapped her head in a urine-soaked sheet and pushed her into the toilet, upside down. Her self-concept will never recover from the nightmares he inflicted on her tender mind. No one can doubt that this kind of hostile and undeserved punishment can be devastating to a youngster. There are, then, many psychological dangers to be avoided in this area.

### TOO EASY

On the other hand, another highly effective way to damage self-esteem is to go to the opposite extreme—avoiding disciplinary control altogether. Many parents create one painful mistake in an attempt to avoid another. When a child knows that he or she has done wrong, has been selfish or offensive to others, that youngster expects the parents to respond appropriately. After all, they are symbols of justice, law, and order which every child loves.

If children are so fond of justice, why is discipline necessary at all? Why can't parents resolve all conflicts by the use of quiet discussions, explanations, and gentle pats on the head? The answer is found in a curious characteristic almost universal in human nature: children care about the issue of "who's toughest."

Whenever a boy or girl moves into a new neighborhood or school, they usually have to fight (either verbally or physically) to establish themselves in the hierarchy of strength. Anyone who understands children knows there is a "top dog" in every group and that there is a poor little defeated pup at the bottom of the heap. And every child in between knows where he or she stands in relation to the others. This respect for strength and courage also makes children want to know how "tough" their leaders are. Whether you are a parent or grandparent, Boy Scout leader, bus driver, Brownie leader, or schoolteacher, sooner or later one of the children under your authority will shake a clenched fist and challenge your leadership. Such a child will convey this message in a defiant manner: "I don't think you are tough enough to make me do what you say."

Most children will occasionally disobey parental instructions for the precise purpose of testing the courage and strength of their leaders. Therefore, boys and girls are often consciously aware of their need to be disciplined for their misbehavior. This fact was illustrated by a father who told me of a time when his five-year-old son was disobeying in a restaurant. The boy was sassing his mother, flipping water on his younger brother, and deliberately making a nuisance of himself. After four warnings, the father took his son by the arm and marched him to the parking lot, where he proceeded to administer a spanking. Watching this episode was a meddling woman who followed them out of the restaurant and into the parking lot. When the spanking began, she shook her finger at the father and screamed, "Leave that boy alone! Turn him loose! If you don't stop, I'm going to call the police!" The five-year-old, who had been crying and jumping, immediately stopped yelling and said to his father in surprise, "What's wrong with that woman, Dad?" He understood the purpose of the discipline, even if the "rescuer" didn't.

When a parent refuses to accept the child's defiant challenge, something changes in their relationship. The youngsters begins to see Mother or Father in a disrespectful light; they are unworthy of allegiance. More important, the child wonders why they would permit such harmful behavior if their love was genuine. The ultimate paradox of childhood is that boys and girls want to be led by their parents but insist that their mothers and fathers earn the right to lead them.

## Guidelines

There will be times, then, when it will be necessary for parents to discipline their children. But what purposes should guide it? What aspects of disobedient behavior are most worthy of parental response? Here are five guidelines which may help establish a reasonable policy of disciplinary control in your future home:

## GUIDELINE ONE—*ADVANCE NOTICE*

It is the responsibility of mothers and fathers to establish reasonable expectations *in advance*. The child should know what is and what is not acceptable behavior *before* that boy or girl is held responsible for the rules. There should never be any ex post facto guilt!

Children profit from a structured environment where the rights of other people (and their own) are protected by certain rules and boundaries. There is great security for children in such a system of loving justice. Conversely, a freewheeling, no-holds-barred atmosphere creates anxiety and frustration for parents and children alike.

## GUIDELINE TWO—*ACCOUNTABILITY*

Once a child understands what is expected, the boy or girl should then be held accountable for behaving accordingly. Sooner or later, a moment of conflict will occur when the youngster will consider the parental wishes and defiantly choose to do the opposite. Having sized up the consequences and considered the costs, this little tiger will dare the parent to accept a challenge. When that nose-to-nose confrontation transpires between a young child and the mother or father, it is *extremely* important (in my view) for the parent to win. Nothing is more destructive to a parent-child relationship than for the adult to disintegrate during the moment of conflict (resorting to tears and screaming and other symptoms of frustration).

When the parent loses dramatically, the child loses even more. Note that I am referring to early disciplinary encounters, when the child is between the ages of two and nine or ten. Compromise and negotiation are more appropriate as the individual grows older, although parental leadership and authority will continue to be valuable until the later teen years.

### GUIDELINE THREE—*IRRESPONSIBILITY*

Children should not be punished for behavior that is not willfully defiant. When they forget to feed the dog or make their bed or take out the trash, when they leave Dad's saw outside in the rain or lose their bicycle, it is important to remember that these behaviors are typical of childhood. We should be gentle as we teach them to do better. If they fail to respond to patient instruction, it then becomes appropriate to administer some well-defined consequences (they may have to work to pay for the item they abused or be deprived of its use, and so forth). However, childish irresponsibility is very different from willful defiance and should be handled more patiently.

### GUIDELINE FOUR—*WELCOME BACK*

After a time of conflict during which the parent has demonstrated the inherent right to lead (particularly if it resulted in tears for the child), the youngster between three and seven may want to be loved and reassured. By all means, open your arms and let the boy or girl come in! Hold them close and tell them of your love. Rock them gently and let them know again why they were punished and how they can avoid the trouble next time. This moment of communication builds love, fidelity, and family unity.

### GUIDELINE FIVE—*CAPABILITY*

Be absolutely sure that your child is capable of delivering what you require. Never punish children for wetting the bed involuntarily or for not becoming potty-trained by one year of age, or for doing poorly in school when they are incapable of certain areas of academic success. These impossible demands put boys and girls in an unresolvable conflict: there is no way out. That condition brings inevitable damage to human emotional apparatus.

I am not recommending that your home be a fearful place for a child to live. I am not suggesting that you give your children a spanking every morning with their ham and eggs, or that you make your boys and girls sit in the living room with their hands folded and their legs crossed. (Children are like clocks; they must be allowed to run.) I am not proposing that you try to make adults out of your offspring so you can impress your grown friends with your parental skill, or that you punish your children inconsistently. I am not suggesting that you insulate your dignity and authority by being cold and unapproachable. These parental tactics do not produce healthy, responsible children.

I am recommending this simple principle: *when you are defiantly challenged by a young child, win decisively.* When your boy or girl asks "Who's in charge," tell him or her. When they mutter "Who loves me?," take them in your arms and surround them with affection. Treat them with respect and dignity, and expect the same in return. Then begin to enjoy the benefits of competent parenthood.

## The Third Beacon:
### RESIST THE TEMPTATION TO GIVE YOUR CHILD TOO MANY TOYS AND GIFTS

Many parents find it difficult, if not impossible, to say no to their children, even when the refusal would be in the best interest of their boys and girls. This is especially true with regard to the persistent demand for toys and games, stuffed animals, three-wheel racers, and the like. Children can become extremely skillful at campaigning for the things they want, and the reluctant parents often surrender to a steady barrage of irritating whines, pleas, and tears. Thus, it takes definite courage to say, "Linda, I know you would like to have Baby Blow Her Nose, but you already have three dolls, and I'm not going to buy you another one."

"DID YOU HEAR ME, MARVIN?"

Some would ask, "And why not, why shouldn't our kids have the things our parents could never afford when we were young?" Certainly, I would not deny boys and girls a reasonable quantity of the things they crave. However, it is possible to give them more than they should have. There are few conditions that destroy a sense of appreciation more than for a child to feel entitled to whatever grabs his fancy at a given moment. It is enlightening to watch such a boy or girl tearing open stacks of presents at a birthday party or perhaps at Christmas time. One after another, the expensive contents are tossed aside with little more than glance. The child's mother is made uneasy by this lack of enthusiasm and gratitude, so she says, "Oh Marvin! Look what it is! It's a little tape recorder! What do you say to Grandmother? Give Grandmother a big hug. Did you hear me, Marvin? Go give Grams a big hug and kiss." Marvin may or may not choose to make the proper noises to Grandmother. His lack of exuberance results from the fact that prizes which are won cheaply are of little value, regardless of the cost to the original purchaser.

## Thanksgiving Dinner

There is another reason young people should be denied some of the things they think they want. Although it sounds contradictory, a parent actually cheats children of pleasure when too much is given. A classic example of this principle occurs in my household each year at Thanksgiving. Our family is blessed with several of the greatest cooks who ever ruled a kitchen, and once a year they do their thing. The traditional Thanksgiving dinner consists of turkey, dressing, cranberries, mashed potatoes, sweet potatoes, peas, hot rolls, two kinds of salad, and six or eight other dishes. Our behavior at this table is disgraceful but wonderful. Everyone eats until he or she is uncomfortable, not saving room for dessert. Then the apple pie, pound cake, and fresh ambrosia are brought to the table. It just doesn't seem possible that we could eat another bite, yet somehow we do. Finally, taut family members begin to stagger away from their plates, looking for a place to fall.

About three o'clock in the afternoon, the internal pressure begins to subside, and someone passes the candy around. As the usual time for the evening meal arrives, no one is hungry, yet we've come to expect three meals a day. Turkey-and-roll sandwiches are constructed and consumed, followed by another helping of pie. By this time, everyone is a bit blank-eyed, absent-mindedly pushing food with their forks and eating what they neither want nor enjoy. This ridiculous ritual continues for two or three days, until the thought of food becomes disgusting.

## Penny the Glutton

To illustrate further, for fourteen years I had a little dog who was never content with the amount of food he was given. He would gulp down his "daily bread" and growl for more, even eating the paper on which the food was served. He was an undeniable glutton. Toward the end of his life, however, he finally got what he had been waiting fourteen years to experience. We had entertained twenty guests for dinner the night before, and had served barbecued spareribs in quantity. The bones and remains from the feast were thrown in a backyard trash can, and somehow Old Penny managed to push over that pail while the family was gone. And what to his wondering eyes should appear but hundreds of rib bones and no one around to bother him!

When we returned several hours later, Penny was lying on the patio with a few stubby bones scattered around his head. Nothing else remained of the garbage he had discovered. Believe it or not, that stupid dog was so full he could not move. His belly was twice its normal size and appeared ready to explode. All four legs were sticking straight out, as if they had no joints. I reached down to pet the poor fellow, and the skin on his distended body was stretched so tight that it felt like concrete. Penny was literally paralyzed by his engorgement, being able to move nothing but his brown eyes. Despite his obvious misery, I thought I detected a subtle smile on his swollen face. I gently picked him up, with his stiff little legs swinging out of control, and put him in his bed. The next evening he would eat nothing and, in fact, was disinterested in his food dish for almost a week.

Obviously, my greedy dog lost his desire for food by the abuse of his appetite, just as my family does every Thanksgiving. My point is that the same disinterest will occur any time needs are completely satiated. *Pleasure only occurs when an intense need is satisfied; if there is no need, there is no enjoyment.* A man who is dying of thirst would give all that he owns for a glass of water, whereas at other times he would pour it on the ground. Thus, worth and value are directly tied to human needs.

## The Joy of Needing

How does this principle relate to children? In this way: If you never permit your boys and girls to want anything... to need anything... they will never enjoy the pleasure of satisfying their desires. If you do not allow them to accumulate an "appetite" for toys and other possessions, they will never experience the thrill of receiving them. If you buy them a tricycle before they can walk, a bicycle before they know how to ride, a car before they can drive, and a diamond ring before they know the value of money, they accept these gifts with little pleasure and less appreciation. How unfortunate that such a child never gets the chance to long for something, dreaming about it at night and plotting for it by day. The youngster might have even gotten desperate enough to work for it! The same possession that brought a yawn could have been a trophy and a treasure. Allow your children the thrill of temporary deprivation of nonessential things; it's far more fun for them, and much less expensive.

Materialism has its place in the life of a child, but it should be kept in reasonable balance with the other influences in the home.

## The Fourth Beacon:
### REMAIN DEEPLY COMMITTED TO YOUR MATE

The greatest gift you can offer your children is a stable and loving home where father and mother are totally committed to one another. Security for children is directly related to stability in the relationship between parents.

During a recent wedding ceremony, the bride and groom rewrote their vows to read "I promise to stay with you for as long as I shall love you." *Love* as they define it is little more than a warm feeling and is destined to collapse.

Stable relationships can't be built on fluctuating emotions. Emotion is needed in human enterprises, but it can't guarantee success on its own. There must be something to back it up. And in the matter of marital relationships, that backup comes from a commitment of the *will*.

If emotion is the caboose of the train of love, then the engine is provided by a person's unyielding determination to make it go. This is the *only* source of long-term stability in marriage.

Every vulnerable little child needs two parents who enjoy this kind of loving relationship. Children thrive on stability, which is a direct product of a long-term commitment.

These four important beacons, then, should guide your own future parenthood: genuine love, consistent discipline, reasonable materialism, and a stable home. Dozens of additional items could be mentioned.

The key to competent parenthood is to be able to get behind the eyes of your children, seeing what they see and feeling what they feel. When they are lonely, they need your company. When they are defiant, they need your help in controlling their impulses. When they are afraid, they need the security of your embrace. When they are curious, they need your patient instruction. When they are happy, they need to share their laughter and joy with those they love.

The parent who intuitively comprehends a child's feelings is in a position to respond appropriately and meet the needs that are apparent. And at this point, raising healthy children becomes a highly developed art, requiring the greatest wisdom, patience, devotion, and love that God has given to us. Certainly, parenthood is a weighty responsibility, but it is worth its price. Besides, nothing worth having comes cheap, anyway.

> Your children are not your children
> They are the sons and daughters of Life's longing
>    for itself.
> They come through you but not from you.
> And though they are with you, yet they belong not
>    to you.
> You may give them your love but not your thoughts
> You may house their bodies but not their souls,
> For their souls dwell in the House of Tomorrow
> Which you cannot visit, not even in your dreams.
> You are the bows from which your children,
>    as living arrows.
> Are sent forth.

—Kahlil Gibran, *The Prophet*

# CARL HALL

E. Carl Hall received his doctorate in education from the University of Oklahoma. He is presently Professor of Consumer and Family Resource Management at Oklahoma State University.

Dr. Hall is author of numerous professional publications and has received several awards for his extensive work in business and economic education. He has spoken before numerous professional organizations and served as a consultant to the President's Committee on Consumer Interests.

In 1970, Dr. Hall was selected one of the Outstanding Young Men in America by the United States Jaycees.

This chapter is an interview between Dr. Carl Hall and two high school students. Jeff and Sheila, both seniors, have been asked to formulate questions to cover things they think most seniors would like to know about money.

# *You and Those Great Big, Beautiful Dollars*

DR. HALL: Misunderstandings about money cause people to work for a lifetime, yet never buy peace of mind or pleasure. There are two major reasons why this is true. First, too many people don't know themselves. Much of the material in this book provides practical ways for you to get to know yourself. It's impossible to be happy or pleased with your life or those around you until you know something about who you are and what you want.

The second reason people fail to buy personal satisfaction in life is their lack of understanding about resources such as money, time, and talent and how these can work for them. These two aspects of management—knowing yourself and understanding resources—are what this chapter is all about.

JEFF AND SHEILA: So many times, when people talk about money, it seems they are relating it to happiness and unhappiness. Why?

DR. HALL: Remember, money is not happiness! It does not provide satisfaction in itself. It is not the goal of work. It is how you make money work for you, not how you work for it. Let's look at Bob and Jim.

Bob and Jim are employed by the same grocery store. They are seniors. Both work only part time. Their jobs and their pay are similar. Bob and Jim have common interests, but Jim always seems to have money and Bob is always broke.

What's the difference? The difference is management. Jim plans carefully, Bob lets things go. He never worries about tomorrow. The question is "Which one is happy with himself?" Who is developing a pattern that could cause problems? They are at an age when it is important to learn planning for the satisfaction of future needs and wants.

Unhappiness is not having what you think will make you happy. But you can increase happiness by planning.

Notice that I haven't used the word budget. Why? Because none of us like to budget. The word has an unpleasant meaning. It sounds like something I don't want to do. But you are planning all the time.

Marsha rides with Amy to the ball game so she can save some gas for a weekend trip. Paul finds a short cut to study for Mr. Simons' test tomorrow. Kim gets an extra helping of meat by going straight to the cook. Everyone is planning all the time. We scheme to make things happen. We do it naturally, so why not use a positive approach to planning? We'll increase the satisfaction from our resources. Planning is a tool to better living. It is a positive force in our lives. It increases our happiness.

JEFF AND SHEILA: You've been talking about wants, and there are a lot of things we would like to have. But how can we plan ahead so, when the time comes, we will be in a position to buy them?

DR. HALL: Let's look at a model for planning. You have spent most of your time in school developing skills that improve your chances for employment. Almost no time, however, has been given to development of other skills that are necessary to buy a good life. Somehow we think if we can earn an income we will buy a life. Look at the divorce rate, drug abuse, suicide, mental illness. You begin to realize that money and things have not "bought the good life" for many people. You realize that there is a gap in your education. You begin to understand. It takes as much knowledge to buy a good life as it does to earn money. Since this is true, it is helpful to look closely at a *planning model*. It can be applied regardless of the level of income or degree of formal education. Three elements define the model:

First, what do you want? Second, what do you have? And third, how can you plan in order to maximize personal satisfaction?

Let's look at the first question:

Have you ever given serious thought to what you want? You say, "Are you kidding? I think about that all the time." Do you really? Or do you think about what someone else has told you you want?

You are now at an age when you need to consider who you really are. This doesn't mean you have to reject your parents or teachers, nor does it mean you have to accept all advice given to you. You may think you want to be free from controls. But freedom brings responsibility. And responsibility comes from searching. Who are you? What do you want?

> Make a list of your wants. Add to it for a week. Now, try to arrange the items in order of importance. What do you want most? What do you want right now? Are there intangible things on your list? Happiness, love, friends?

Use your list to determine your values. For example, you say you want an education, yet most of your time is spent socializing. There isn't anything wrong with wanting to socialize or desiring an education. But notice the inconsistencies or differences between things you have written down and the way you spend your time, money, and ability. It should be emphasized again that there is not a right or wrong in wanting one thing over another. But your behavior may indicate one want while your actions are saying you want something else. This usually leads to conflict in your approach to getting what you want.

One reason a lot of us don't accomplish what we want

is because we say we want one thing, but our lives indicate we want another. Until we get our act together, we will experience feelings of anger and frustration.

In a quiet, serious time, when you are all alone, what do you really want? You will have difficulty enjoying what you have until you realize that your wants are many, perhaps unlimited. What was that? Remember, wants are endless. When one is satisfied, two more take the place of that one. You are hungry, so you eat. That want is satisfied. A few hours later, you're hungry again—this time for something different. In fact, if you don't control your eating, you will gain weight and have a new set of problems.

Satisfaction of all of your appetites is impossible. Example? Your new outfit for a party serves its purpose, but another is needed for the next party. You could buy and buy and buy. Or you want another chromed piece for your car engine. It would run better and faster. It would look great. After that piece, there is still another you want. When the car is finally fixed up, it's time to trade it in on a nicer model.

You see, then, wants can be unlimited. This simply means we are constantly trying to satisfy an endless variety of wants, but our resources—money, time, talent—are limited. Therefore, choices need to be made. This brings us back to the first question. What do we want? Which wants are most important? We seem anxious to address the questions of *who I am* and *what do I want* as we make decisions.

JEFF AND SHEILA: So you're saying it's a matter of using our resources to supply our wants. Right?

DR. HALL: Yes. This brings us to the second point— what do you have?

**Write a list of all of your present resources.**

Understanding that resources such as money, time, and ability are limited presents an interesting and sometimes frustrating problem. *How can we take limited resources and make them provide answers for unlimited wants?*

A lot of students get bored with school. Well, the next time you are bored, take a newspaper and look through the want-ad section. What jobs are available that you could fill right now? How much do these jobs pay? Do they pay enough to provide the type of living you think you could be happy with?

A teacher had students complete this exercise one day. Not one student found the right job! None of the jobs could provide the amount of income necessary to buy the life style they wanted. This exercise made school and learning more important to most of the students. Learning is for you, not for the teacher. You are developing skills that will make a better life. Once you understand resources are limited, the question is: How can I maximize them in order to satisfy my wants? *Planning* is the answer.

Planning the use of resources involves recognizing strengths and weaknesses and using all of the available resources. For example, you might seriously study how to buy a used car. You could save hundreds of dollars and make driving a more enjoyable experience. On the other hand, your lack of information could mean you end up buying one lemon after another, and this might lead you to believe that everyone selling used cars is out to beat the consumer.

Suddenly, the light dawns. In this deal, you are the one who is most interested in whether you get the best from your time, money, or ability. But ours is a unique-market system. Buyer and seller have different motivations. The used car dealer is trying to make the greatest possible profit. At the same time, you are after the best possible car for the least amount of money. You and the seller come together at a price which should be reasonable for both.

That car dealer has had years of experience. He knows the psychology of the market. You have almost no understanding of how the market works. Granted, you know something about cars, but sometimes you let the shine and desire for wheels go to your head. You don't get the most transportation for the money.

You must know what you want and how to use limited resources to get it. This will help maximize your satisfaction. It also points up the fact that you need to research the market before rushing into a purchase. The fact is that you cannot spend money or time twice.

What? You mean the used car you bought for $795 didn't cost $795? No, it cost the down payment on a new car. It cost the trip to Europe. It cost a cheaper car and a summer vacation trip on the coast. The $795 cannot be spent twice. Alternative choices make up the real cost of the car.

Wow, what an idea! This makes it exciting to think about what you buy. The hamburger you bought yesterday didn't really cost seventy-five cents. It cost a gallon of gas. A part of a show ticket or a paperback book. It cost the other choices you could have made with the seventy-five cents. That also means you can weight the choice in terms of the satisfaction it gives.

What about satisfaction from other choices? Would the choice of the car or the hamburger give you greater satisfaction? What are the alternative costs of the car or hamburger? Obviously, the more dollars you spend, the more significant alternative costs become.

For the next thirty days, keep a record of the money you spend (only as much detail as you like).

At the end of that thirty-day period, compare it to your list of wants. Are there differences? Are they reasons for unhappiness? Could you correct them?

DR. HALL: Now that you have studied your records, you are ready to build a spending plan. That's the third element of a successful economic life. The plan is built around what you are doing already, plus changes that you think should be made. The plan will make it much easier to accomplish your goals. The plan will need to be changed from time to time. You may get more money, or unexpected expenses may occur. This kind of spending plan has worked for many other young people. In fact, it has been so successful that it provides a model for spending throughout life. Of course, it is adjusted frequently. It becomes a management tool, not a financial straitjacket.

JEFF AND SHEILA: Most of us have had some experience with borrowing, as from parents or friends. It seems like borrowing can really get you into trouble. But also isn't it all right to borrow for some things? When is it wise to borrow? And from where?

DR. HALL: Lend me a hundred dollars! Sound silly? Not at all. It is a question of trust. Trust in my ability and desire to repay the hundred dollars. Banks and other "money stores" do business on the basis of trust. Sometimes they want more than your word. They may want the title to your car. This insures repayment of the loan. Even so, money places operate their businesses on the trust they have in people.

Does *money store* sound like a peculiar name for a bank, credit union, or small-loan company? Think. It really is a money store. It is a place where people save and borrow together. When you go to the money store the lender asks about your Character, Capacity, and Capital.

Character says, yes, I'll repay the loan. Will you really try? Have you repaid others? Do you do things when you say you will? All this makes a difference. Will the lender lend the money to you?

Capacity says, will you have enough money to repay the loan? Are you earning regularly? Have you saved up any money? Could someone else pay if you don't? (This person is called a co-signer.) Let's face it, to borrow money, you should be able and willing to pay it back, and within a specified period of time.

Capital says, what do I have that's valuable? What do I own? My savings account! Stereo! Car! Can I make money work?

Yes, you can have a checking or savings account. You can borrow money for a car, vacation trip, doctor bills. But all for a fee. What fee? Well, you may have a checking account that costs ten cents a check. Or you pay interest for a loan. The banker has to earn, too.

We all have different needs and different assets. Not everybody pays the same. Remember those three C's? The less trust a person has in you, the more it costs. That is why a good credit rating is so all-important.

Other money stores also offer services. Credit unions are unique types of money stores. They are money co-ops, operated by a group of people who borrow and save together. These are people who have some common interests. They work at the same place or do something together.

Credit unions usually have better interest rates on loans

than commercial or savings banks. For example, 1 percent per month on the amount owed. This includes insurance on the loan. Generally, no penalties are charged for early repayment. And if you have a savings account with them, your interest is usually only 8 or 9 percent per month. New-car loans are sometimes even lower.

Most money stores charge extra even if you pay early. Does that sound strange? Maybe it's because most lenders (except credit unions) apply a rule you may never have heard. It is called "the rule of 78s." This is a complicated rule—and one that runs the cost of a loan up. For example, using the rule of 78s, a one-year loan paid off in six months would have almost three-quarters of the total interest charged to the borrower. Shouldn't the borrower pay only half the interest? Not on the rule of 78s. This penalizes the borrower for paying early. The lender thinks it's all right. He has additional paperwork.

All of this means that shopping for money is very important. It is foolish to spend time finding the best price on a car, then pay an extra $500 in financing charges. The more you borrow, the more shopping you should do for money. Once you've settled on a loan, read the contract agreement carefully—before you sign it. It protects the lender, not you. It is filled with a lot of small print that makes you responsible for added costs if you cannot pay. It doesn't give you much protection. The product you buy should work. But the lender may not care whether it works or not. So read, then write your name. If a deal is so good it won't wait, it may be too good.

Here's a story one student told me: "My father says if somebody wants to sell you something right now and they are trying to get you to buy it this very minute, watch out! This is

what they call the 'hard sell' and
how they do it is to get you pan-
icky. You know—you've got to decide right now, and if you don't,
somebody else will get it. Whenever you meet one of these charac-
ters, turn around and run as fast as
you can."

Can you give some examples of
your own experiences?

DR. HALL:   It is very important to be careful when borrowing at a small-loan company. These companies are useful. But often the first hook of easy credit carries a high
price. Interest rates will vary from 18 to 36 percent! It
depends on the size and time the loan runs. Small-loan
companies usually make smaller loans than commercial or
savings banks. So their costs are higher.

Shop carefully and know what you are buying before
you borrow money. You won't be sorry.

JEFF AND SHEILA:   We have heard the terms *overinsured*
and *underinsured*. How do you know how much insurance
to buy? Are there things we should know? What about different kinds of insurance?

DR. HALL:   You've heard the term *I'll bet you!* Boys bet
on ballgames, on fights, on who's right. Girls are more in-
clined to guess who will date whom or how long a new
recording group will stay together. We all like to think
about possibilities of some event occurring or not occurring.
For example, the odds are better than two to one that if
you ask six friends, two of them will have the same birth

month. But what does all this have to do with risk and insurance?

Believe it or not, there are people called actuaries who make money figuring out the chances of something happening or not happening. Based on actual experience and mathematical possibilities, they can accurately predict how many men or women of a certain age will die this year. This is referred to as objective risk. These data are used in establishing costs of life insurance.

An actuary may know how many seventeen-year-old females or males will die this year, but there are still unknowns. They don't know *which* seventeen-year-olds. This is called subjective risk.

Does all this sound morbid? It isn't intended to be, and it is very important. It forms the basis on which you make decisions about how you will meet risk. The loss of a stereo by fire or theft. A car accident. The loss of an eye. Premature death. These represent a thousand and one things which may or may not happen. You see, once you were conceived in your mother's womb, you started facing risks. So the question is, how will you meet the risks?

All losses have one thing in common. Things are not the same after loss. The fender you smashed: it was fixed well enough, but it is not the same fender. So, some value of the fender was replaced—money was paid for someone to rebuild it. The same is true with life.

When a parent dies, the person cannot be brought back to life. But the money value of that parent's life can be restored. A life insurance policy pays so the family can continue to live. You can stay in school to complete your education. In other words, even though that parent died, a part of his or her income is paid to the family. It helps those who depended on them.

Insurance, whether on life, property, or health, is designed to provide financial help in time of need. This is a sharing process. Those who buy life insurance are pooling money in a life insurance company. They agree if a person in the group dies, money will be taken from the pool to pay for the needs of the family. This is an important idea. Your understanding of it helps determine how much and what type of insurance you buy.

There are two major things which determine how much insurance you will buy: (1) Whether you think you will be the one to lose, and (2) The type of risk-taker you are. All of this may seem strange, but it is tremendously important. Your responsibilities to others are different, and insurance salesmen use psychology. They want to know what kind of risk-taker you are. So, you need to know what types of insurance are available and what your financial needs are.

Remember, your attitudes toward risk are very important. You can always learn about life, or automobile, or health, or renters' insurance. But it's tough to know which kind does what. Protection is personal and should fit your specific needs. If you know yourself and your needs, you will be an intelligent consumer of insurance protection.

JEFF AND SHEILA: A friend of ours with a part-time job is already paying taxes. We pay sales tax, and things like that. But income tax for a high school student? What do you think about this?

DR. HALL: You're right. A high school student who is working will pay income tax.

Mark began working part time when he was a junior. He worked fifteen hours a week at minimum wage. And he almost came apart when he picked up his first paycheck. "I thought I was making minimum wage!" he stormed. "You are!" retorted his boss. "Mark," he said, "let me show you the wide, wonderful world of taxes." Federal and state taxes. Tax—tax—tax! Mark made the connection. Highways, parks, schools, and national defense didn't just drop out of heaven one dark night. Mark even saw a relationship between vandalism at school, which he was now helping pay for, and *his* tax dollars. "I'm contributing to this school in a financial way through tax dollars. I guess I better show a little more respect. After all, I wouldn't go out and cut up the seats in the car I paid for. So, I better watch what happens to my school." Mark really took a giant step. A large number of us don't seem to relate all of these things.

With payroll deductions, Mark learned that he must file an income-tax form at the end of the year. In fact, Mark was introduced to a number of ideas rather quickly. When he started to work, he was given a W4 form. Now he was asking, "What's a W4 form? What does it mean?" He was informed that it meant several things. One thing was that he would show the number of "personal exemptions" he wanted to claim. That's one thing the W4 form means. But that's not all. The employer has a huge table provided by the Internal Revenue Service. This table shows how much he should withhold from Mark's salary. He would base it on the amount of income earned, the number of exemptions claimed. So the more exemptions he claims, the less his employer will withhold. Since Mark is single and has no other dependents, he can only claim one exemption on the W4. He also claims only one when he files his return at the end of the year.

These early experiences with employment and taxes were not only new to Mark, they fascinated him. In fact, he became so interested he offered to help his parents file their federal income tax report. From all this he learned a lot about recordkeeping and responsibility to prove deductions. It was amazing how much could be deducted if they kept records. Medical expenses, interest paid on loans, taxes paid to state and local agencies, contributions, and a large range of miscellaneous deductions could be counted.

> Call your Internal Revenue Service and request copies of "Teaching Taxes Program." It is provided by the United States Treasury Department. You will gain appreciation of how tax money is used.

JEFF AND SHEILA: Are there some things you'd like to tell us about investing?

DR. HALL: Yes. We're all interested in saving and placing our money where it will earn more money.

Benjamin Franklin didn't have a corner on saving money. A penny saved, earns. Either you make money work, or you work for money.

A stockbroker in the Midwest had a customer who wanted to invest $2000. The story starts in the late 1950s. The investor defined his objective. He wanted to take a reasonable risk in the hope his investment would grow rapidly.

With this in mind, the broker recommended Xerox. In 1958, the dry photocopy process was unproved and represented speculative, high-risk venture. The investor was willing to take the risk. But, would you believe, the Xerox stock costing $2000 is now worth in excess of $600,000!

This is the kind of rags-to-riches story we like. But even if it's a true story, which it is, there are some other truths we need to know about investing. For every unknown company like Xerox which has become a major power in the marketplace, there are many that failed and cost the investors money.

Here's the dilemma. Is the stock market unsafe? Should

I always be afraid of losing money? Are there places where I should invest, things I could buy which will be certain to increase in value?

Each of these questions is important. But first and most important is the development of a style of living. A style you are comfortable with. This will include a number of such necessary things as housing, transportation, clothes, food. It should also include some provision for uncertainty.

Could you afford to lose your property? Are there others who depend on you for financial support? Does this mean you need to buy some type of life insurance? Is there some money set aside for use in an emergency? Once these things are taken care of, you should be able to make additional dollars work.

The stock market provides a viable outlet. But no plan will make money by itself. That is, you must study and work your plan. One of the first things you should decide is how much risk you want to take. To illustrate, if you buy stock, do you want to speculate—take a lot of risk? Or, do you want to buy something that may grow safely, steadily? How comfortable are you with risk? If you buy art, do you want to go with the young, aspiring artist who might someday be great? Or do you want to reduce your risk by selecting paintings or sculpture created by a well-known artist? There is an investment for every level of risk.

After you think about the amount of risk you will take, select an investment that interests you. Next, become a student. For example, if you are interested in real estate, start by learning all you can about particular types of real estate. Or, maybe you like antique cars. How does their value fluctuate? Where is the best place to buy them? How can you restore their luster and increase their value? Maybe you are interested in jewelry. What types of stones have increased value? Where are the markets in fine jewelry? How can you learn more about jewelry? These and hundreds of other questions are important to your success as an investor.

Not many people make money by accident. You hear about the gambler who won big at the race track. (Remember the princess whose pumpkin turned into a golden carriage?) All of us fantasize things like that, but most individuals who make their money work have become students of some specific thing. They put their knowledge to work along with their money.

There are books filled with information on the stock market, the commodities market, land investment, bonds, antique furniture, foreign art, new inventions, jewelry, and other things. You should remember, however, there is no quick, easy road to financial success. The road is filled with chuckholes and detours. But, if you are persistent and willing to learn, financial success can be yours. It comes to those who work for it.

One last word on investing. Never forget why you are investing. If you are making money just to be making money, there is little reward. If you are making money work in order to enjoy a better life, the trip is worth every bump and turn. You will lose some and win some, but over the long run, you will be pleased with your effort.

JEFF AND SHEILA: After we settle down, like marriage and getting a permanent job, a lot of our money will go for housing. Do you have any suggestions on this?

DR. HALL: Yes, young people today face many problems when it comes to housing. What type, where, and how much will it cost?

You will be amazed at the many alternatives. Most of us think in traditional terms. An apartment, a mobile home, a house, a condominium. Other options? Modular housing is one option, and it's a fascinating concept. Why couldn't a place to live grow with you as your family grows? Then it could be reduced in size as your situation changes. Too much to hope for? Not at all. In fact, there are unique experimental designs being created as you read this. This means you can be more creative as you anticipate housing needs for the future.

Meanwhile, back to your first home away from home. It is safe to say that most young people will spend time in an apartment before they move to some other type of housing. This raises questions about how to shop for and wisely use an apartment as a home. With this in mind, let's start where the action is. Can you read the lease agreement? Is it a bunch of words or do you understand your obligations? Are there parts which should be changed before you sign it? What about pets?

Next, you should think about the condition of the apartment. Will you get your deposit back? Landlords may keep your deposit if there is any visible damage, whether you caused it or not. Is the stove dirty? Why is that hole in the bedroom wall? All of these defects should be noted by your landlord *before* you move in. (Ask him to put it in writing.) This protects your deposit.

Other questions: Are utilities included or do you pay your own bills? Can the landlord raise the rent anytime he wishes? Can he enter the apartment to inspect it anytime? And how long will it take him to return your deposit? Questions, questions, questions. It is better to ask them before you move in than to wonder what has happened when you move out.

Apartments are excellent for many people. But what about those who want some other type of living arrangement? Housing is so expensive. Utilities cost a lot. It's difficult to move even if you want to. Maybe a condominium is the answer. You don't have to cut the grass, yet you actually own the unit you live in. This provides income-tax deductions for interest and property taxes. At the same time it is similar to apartment-type living. Of course, anytime you own something, you have to sell it before you are free of responsibility. Move from the apartment—no worries. Move from a condominium or home, you must sell it. Of course, ownership usually means saving dollars.

There are other things to consider when buying a condominium or home. What about furniture, draperies, lawn, trees, and other responsibilities that go with home ownership? These responsibilities can be fun, but they mean work. So, maybe the answer is a house trailer, or motor home, or a bedroom with relatives.

Whatever you select, your choice should meet not only your physical but also your emotional, psychological, and financial needs. Living with parents after you are married may be expensive, not in dollars, but in tension and strained relationships. A house trailer may be great in certain situations, but it could be a difficult way to save money.

The message is clear. Think about who you are and what you want. Then find the best possible answer. If you go at this intelligently, living will be fun. It is surprising how the smallest apartment can become a palace if we understand ourselves and define our goals.

Happiness cannot be found in things. It is found in being pleased with life and making those nearby happy, too. Individuals who radiate excitement and joy have found a peace and pleasure in themselves that speaks to the whole world. So, a house is not a home, but almost any place you live can be made one.

JEFF AND SHEILA: We think most high school seniors want to make a valuable contribution with their lives. Some of us have been raised in the church, so we know about giving money to charities and and worthwhile organizations. But sometimes it doesn't seem like it's really that important. Do you have any ideas or tips on giving?

DR. HALL:   You are wise to think about giving some of your money. Your life is yours to build. And it will be rewarding to look at yourself with confidence and be able to say, "I took what I had, and did well with it." Possession of things never will provide satisfaction. True satisfaction comes from giving, and that is learned from sharing with others. Those who hold everything they have are some of the most frightened people on earth. And empty. Those who have learned the joy of giving are some of the most fulfilled people you will ever meet.

What does all this mean? It simply means that for real joy, each person must keep attitudes toward things in proper perspective.

All the material possessions you can imagine, all the wise money management you can learn, are not enough unless you are willing to know who you are and what you want. Don't worry about mistakes. They are our greatest teacher. Consider what you have and share some of it for a rich, full life. There will be no regrets.

# RICHARD BOLLES

Richard Nelson Bolles has been called "probably the most widely read and respected leader in the career/lifework planning fields." He is the author of the best-selling books *What Color Is Your Parachute?: A Practical Manual for Job-Hunters and Career Changers, The Three Boxes of Life, and How to Get Out of Them, The Quick Job-Hunting Map,* and co-author with John C. Crystal of *Where Do I Go from Here with My Life?* He is the director of the National Career Development Project of United Ministries in Higher Education.

# *You and What You Will Do*

After high school, what will you do with yourself? Continue your education? Find a job? Or just drift? Which one is for you?

On first thought, perhaps the most attractive of these three worlds may be drifting. You've had it with school.

College? That might seem like a sentence to prison.

Work? Maybe you don't have the foggiest idea what you want to do. Besides, you already had a taste of work. McDonald's... pumping gas... carrying papers... camp counselor... babysitting. From these brief encounters with work, it may not be for you. Not full-time, not yet. Well, that's what happened with Don.

## The World of Drifting

On Don's report card his teachers had repeatedly written "Bright student. Not working to full capacity." Don had long since learned to shrug this off.

After graduation he decided to look for a job. He didn't particularly care what, so he checked with his friends, looked in the ads, even went for a couple of disappointing interviews. But the job opportunities turned out to be discouraging, and he finally decided nothing interested him.

Don's parents said, "We know it takes a while to decide what direction you're going." So with room and board assured, Don stayed around, doing nothing. At first it was fun. Like an extended vacation. Some of his friends decided to take the summer off before they went looking for a job. Others going to college were there, too. Lots of clowning around. Lots of laughs.

But then fall came. Some friends left for college. Those taking a job were busy, too. And the only ones around now were two or three of his cronies who, like Don, had decided to drift. Suddenly, things weren't quite so much fun. Life was boring. At home, his parents began to get less patient and understanding. His mother began hinting. Don knew what she was doing. A newspaper neatly turned to the want-ads. Magazines opened to articles on unemployment. Pamphlets. Everywhere, subtle suggestions.

His father, never much for tact, turned the dinner conversation to "those no-good bums who think the country owes them a living." This was always good for a half-hour argument and made mealtime more and more dreaded each day. Eventually Don decided arguments were useless, so he allowed his father's remarks to go right on by.

Then came the holidays and the return of college friends. It was a big relief as Don threw himself into the parties, the get-togethers. But attempts to recapture that old "high school feeling" seemed more and more futile. Their talk was different. It was hard for him to join in. His friends were "in" with each other. And he was "out." So that's how it was with drifting. Fine for a while, but more and more Don realized this was no permanent solution.

Some people are able to stay in the world of drifting all their lives. But for most of us, drifting won't last. So let's examine the other options.

> Ten years from now, where would you like to be with your life?

## The World of Further Education

In America, it used to be taken for granted that any sensible high school senior with halfway decent grades would automatically go to college. In 1967–1968, 63 percent of all high school graduates went on to college, and more than half of these finished. The assumption: getting that college degree would mean a better job, plus more earnings.

Today this isn't necessarily true. Having a college degree does not automatically guarantee a job. Many college graduates, particularly in the humanities and teaching professions, cannot find a job in the fields for which they trained. And in many cases, college graduates settle for a much lower-paying job than they anticipated. (Books such as The Case against College by Caroline Bird, and The Over-Educated American by Richard Freeman, question whether every high school senior with decent grades should automatically go to college.)

Many others are challenging the idea of "automatic" further education. Because the job market has changed in the last decade, the wise graduate will make his or her decision on reasons important to him or herself.

Since the "life is better if you go to college" argument is questionable, what are some good reasons for further education?

Here are a few worth considering:

1. *To enlarge mental, emotional, and spiritual horizons.*

As you grew from infancy to adolescence, your horizons expanded. First, your mother's arms defined the borders of your awareness. Then those borders expanded to include your room, the house, the yard, the neighborhood, town, countryside, nations, world, universe. One reason for education beyond high school is to help those horizons grow still larger.

2. *To learn the limits of knowledge.*

There are certain things which our senses, our eyes, our ears can tell us. Other things they cannot tell. Example? The room you're sitting in is filled with sounds your ears cannot hear. But if you have a radio, the sounds become evident. The radio does not create those sounds, it only "brings them in."

Again, the room in which you are sitting is filled with pictures your eyes cannot see. But if you have a television, the pictures become evident. In this case, too, the television does not create those pictures, it only converts electronic signals into pictures you can see.

One reason for seeking further education is to learn more about what else our senses can detect. What are the limits of our knowledge?

Are there other "realities" in the universe which our senses cannot comprehend because we have not yet discovered anything to bring those realities in? Any possibilities occur to you?

### 3. *Learning how to think.*

Newspapers, magazines, books, the marketplace, television create a constant bombardment of facts and statistics. Your high school experience should have taught you how to evaluate, how to weigh information. But do you need more help? Do you know enough to evaluate your interests; to follow your curiosity; to use your thinking processes effectively; to follow your logic; to analyze; to deal with your intuition?

### 4. *Education for coping with change. And understanding those things which do not change.*

Ten, fifteen years from now we will be living in a world markedly different from today's world. One purpose of further education is to master more tools for dealing with these changes. But as we develop our ability to cope with changes of all kinds, we must look to another fact. Some things do not change, even when we wish they would. There is a kind of stubborn consistency in our world, most of it rooted in our human nature. This, too, we need to know more about. So every one of us will require better tools for dealing with nonchanging factors. To understand the changing and nonchanging may be another valid reason for more education.

### 5. *Further stimulation for mind, heart, and will.*

Each of us has not only a body but also a mind, a heart, a will. We think, we feel, and we also choose. Another purpose for further education could be that we feel some part of us did not receive all it needed while we were in high school. Maybe we would like to examine further the question "What is truth?" Or delve into key ideas of Western or Eastern thought. Or consider certain fundamental bases of civilization.

Stimulation for the heart includes emotion, feeling, intuition, love, hate, beauty. What attracts us? What repels us? Did we learn enough about these things in high school?

Development of the will may include conscience, morality, values, ethics, perfection, righteousness. To learn more about these limitless concepts may be sufficient reason alone to seek further education.

*6. A chance to meet other people with similar interests.*

Alice loved psychology. In high school, she not only wanted to learn more about psychology, she enjoyed being with other people who enjoyed psychology. For that reason she went on to college. Mark had a special interest in all kinds of people. He enjoyed people, enjoyed dating, enjoyed crowds. He saw college primarily as a way of meeting new people, new girls, joining in talk sessions with different groups. Many high school seniors choose college for people-reasons, first.

*7. To polish skills in preparation for a particular field, a line of work, a job.*

This is, of course, the principal reason why most high school seniors go on to college. They want to prepare for the world of work. This may mean a vocational/technical institute, a community college, a big university. It may mean correspondence school, the armed forces, adult education programs in the community, an apprenticeship, or college courses offered on television.

For some occupations, extended education is essential: the professions—doctors, lawyers, clergy, architects; the sciences—engineers, physicists, chemists; specialists of all types—beauticians, key-punch operators, executive secretaries, diesel mechanics, hospital technicians.

Do you know about DOT? It is a three-volume set of books called *The Dictionary of Occupational Titles*. More than 20,000 jobs are listed in the DOT. They divide into the following categories:

a. Jobs which can be done by anyone with elementary skills, and without further education;

b. Jobs done by anyone with elementary skills, plus minimum training on the job;

c. Jobs requiring more extensive training.

If you are going on to any form of education beyond high school, it is important that you decide first what kind of work you would like. If your decision fits one of the first two categories, this does not mean you should not go to college. You may still choose advanced education for personal reasons.

8. *To improve personality and develop individuality.*

Most high school juniors and seniors want to know: Who am I? Why am I here? What's unusual or unique about me? What do I want to accomplish? What is the meaning of my life? Some are content to let these answers unfold gradually. Others can't wait. They want to know immediately. Further education for them is a matter of self-improvement and the unfolding of their uniqueness.

After you have weighed these eight reasons, you can decide for yourself whether you want further education. The benefits aren't the same for everyone. And certainly, not everyone who goes to college discovers him- or herself or finds the meaning of life. For many, college is a repeat of what may have been a poor high school experience— difficult, lonely, and unfulfilling. Others find it exciting, helpful, and meaningful.

The important key to your fulfillment, whether it be in

further education or work, is the extent to which you involve yourself in the experience. Both worlds require a big part of you to be involved in order to achieve self-fulfillment.

Your school counselor, parents, minister, priest, or rabbi can help advise which alternatives may be best for you. Some of you may have already had experience working, and have liked it. Others of you may not have worked at all, so far; entering the world of work will be a new experience for you.

What will the world of work be like? Regardless of what kind of job you take, you'll find there are four kinds of learnings you'll need to master. And because it's learning, work will not be all that different from school—but here you'll learn on the job.

Let's look at how Pat and Bill dealt with these four kinds of learnings. They both graduated from high school last year and decided to try the world of work. This was the first job for both of them. They decided to apply together for jobs downtown in a restaurant where they had seen a "Help Wanted" sign in the window. They were both hired there, she as a waitress, he as a busboy. They were given quite a few instructions by their boss on their first day at work. They listened very attentively, memorizing the obvious sorts of things, but taking notes about anything they thought they might not remember.

There were two other waitresses and one other busboy working at the restaurant. Pat and Bill spent the morning watching them, and they learned quite a lot about their respective jobs. Just before lunch, they went to the boss and asked him several questions they had jotted down during the morning, about things they had seen the waitreses or busboy do that had puzzled them. After the boss answered, they went to work. For the first week or two, Pat turned to the other waitresses and Bill to the other busboy any time a customer asked a question they could not answer. They were careful to thank the waitress or the busboy each time they got an answer. Pat and Bill were dealing with the first kind of learning that you have on any job: How do you find out what's happening? If you don't know, you are going to be in big trouble. You find out what's happening by the same process Pat and Bill used: listening, observing, and politely asking questions.

Once they knew what was happening, Pat and Bill took particular care to observe the waitress who was obviously the best. They tried to watch the kind of rhythm she established with her work, how she paced herself, and how she dealt with the customers. They noticed she concentrated on getting her work done, but she never got so focused on the work that she couldn't take time to be pleasant with the customers. Besides studying her, Pat and Bill also asked the boss once or twice a week, for the first month, if there was anything he saw them do that they might do better.

In all of this, they were trying to learn how to survive on the job. Getting hired for a job is only half the battle. Holding on to that job is the other half. Whenever the other employees reminisced about employees who used to be there but were laid off or fired, Pat and Bill would ask them why. And any time they heard their boss get upset about something, they listened very carefully. They realized that doing the job according to his standards was the secret to survival.

After learning what level of work they needed to do in order to survive on the job, Pat and Bill asked themselves what kind of skills they were using in their respective jobs. Pat realized that she was becoming skilled at dealing with people. She found that she enjoyed helping them decide

what to order, and talking with them. Bill found his satisfaction as busboy was in figuring out faster or more efficient
ways of getting the work done. Both Pat and Bill were
learning—in all of this—how to get some sense of meaning, or personal mission, out of what would otherwise be
regarded as a humdrum job. They set their own goals for
what they wanted to get out of a job, in terms of their own
personal development and job satisfaction. Once you have
decided you really know what's happening, and that you
are going to survive on that job, it is very important to
decide what is giving you your sense of meaning there. And
then to concentrate on that—while not neglecting the other
things that need to get done.

Pat and Bill were receiving compliments from the waitresses and the boss about what a nice job they were doing.
Such over-all, general kinds of compliment were very encouraging. But what Pat and Bill paid particular attention
to was how they were doing in the particular skill areas
they chose to work on. Both of them were concentrating
on their effectiveness—not comparing themselves with
others, but comparing themselves this month with themselves last month. And not just looking at their over-all
effectiveness but more particularly at their effectiveness in
the one small area they had chosen to work on. This was
their fourth kind of learning—how to increase their effectiveness. It is the kind of learning that you will need to
master, regardless of what kind of job you take.

As was true for Pat and Bill, these are the four problems
you will need to wrestle with:

*First:* What is happening there, particularly in terms of
what is expected of you.

*Second:* You will need to consider how you can guarantee your survival in this job.

*Third:* You must plan how to make your job have meaning for you in terms of your own personal agenda and personal development.

*Fourth:* How can you increase your effectiveness as time goes on?

Having identified the major problems, here's the important question:

## How Do You Decide What You Will Do?

One way of deciding is to see what is available. Try to turn up the names of employers who have a vacancy, and then go to see if they will give you an interview. You can do this by faithfully looking at the want ads in the newspaper, haunting employment agencies, telling all your friends that you're looking for a job, and visiting plants, companies, or stores looking for work. If you're not too choosy and you're willing to sit in a lot of personnel offices filling out application forms, you'll get a job. But keep in mind that there are lots of people who, twenty years after high school graduation, are still working at their first jobs. They let the first vacancy they found decide for them. Years later, they were still doing the same kind of work as when they started. Somewhere, somehow, they lost the dream they once had, that they were entitled to something more fulfilling, more true to the talents they had been given.

On the other hand, you may hold a succession of jobs in a relatively short period of time, quitting each one because it wasn't quite what you had in mind. It is not difficult to find a young adult who is three to five years out of high school and has already had ten or so jobs. Those people are usually hoping that life will make a decision for them— and accidentally drop them into precisely the right slot.

Well, suppose it doesn't. Or suppose that right now you decide you're not going to go this aimless, wandering route. You want to choose carefully what it is that they will do. You want to be the decision-maker for your own life. How do you go about doing that? There are three basic decisions facing you:

1. What are the things I most enjoy doing, and what skills do they require?

2. Where, or in the service of what, would I like to use those skills?

3. How do I identify those places where I would be the happiest and be able to do my most effective work? And how do I get hired there?

Let's have a further look at these three important questions:

1. *What are the things I most enjoy doing and what skills does it take to do them?*

  a. List on a separate sheet of paper all the things you have most enjoyed doing, as far back as you can remember. When did you enjoy yourself most? At school, in your spare time, with hobbies or volunteer work, in work experiences—where did you feel best? Ask your parents, brothers, sister, or friends when they noticed you enjoying yourself.

  b. From this list, choose several favorites (up to fifteen). Write a paragraph description for each experience.

  c. Then rank each paragraph or experience in order of enjoyment for you. For example, if you had fifteen paragraphs, use #1 for the most enjoyable, #15 for the most boring one.

  d. Go down the list and, under each experience or time you were doing something you enjoyed, color in with a pen or pencil whenever you used a par-

ticular skill. Example: If #1 was "learned to ride a
bicycle," then your list would look like this:

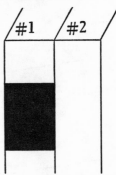

3. Building
4. Operating tools
5. Operating machinery
6. Operating equipment
7. Showing manual or finger dexterity
8. Handling with precision or speed

# Job Skills Inventory

| | 1. | 2. | 3. | 4. | 5. | 6. | 7. | 8. | 9. | 10. | 11. | 12. | 13. | 14. | 15. |
|---|---|---|---|---|---|---|---|---|---|---|---|---|---|---|---|
| | | | | | | | | | | | | | | | |

**I. USING MY HANDS**

1. Assembling
2. Constructing
3. Building
4. Draftsmanship
5. Operating machinery
6. Operating equipment
7. Showing manual or finger dexterity
8. Handling with precision or speed

_____

_____

_____

_____

_____

_____

_____

_____

_____

_____

_____

_____

_____

9. Fixing or
   repairing
10. Other:

II. *USING MY BODY*
11. Muscular
    coordination
12. Being physically
    active
13. Doing outdoor
    activities
14. Other:

III. *USING WORDS*
15. Reading
16. Copying
17. Writing or
    communicating
18. Speaking or
    talking
19. Teaching,
    training
20. Editing

## Job Skills Inventory (continued)

| 1. | 2. | 3. | 4. | 5. | 6. | 7. | 8. | 9. | 10. | 11. | 12. | 13. | 14. | 15. |
|---|---|---|---|---|---|---|---|---|---|---|---|---|---|---|
| | | | | | | | | | | | | | | |
| | | | | | | | | | | | | | | |

21. Memory for words
22. Other:

IV. *USING MY SENSES
(EYES, EARS, NOSE,
TASTE, TOUCH)*

23. Observing,
    surveying
24. Examining or
    inspecting
25. Diagnosing,
    determining
26. Showing attention
    to detail

_____

_____

_____

_____

_____

_____

_____

_____

_____

_____

_____

_____

_____

_____

27. Other:

## V. *USING NUMBERS*

28. Taking inventory
29. Counting
30. Calculating, computing
31. Keeping financial records, bookkeeping
32. Managing money
33. Developing a budget
34. Number memory
35. Rapid manipulation of numbers
36. Other:

## VI. *USING INTUITION*

37. Showing foresight

# Job Skills Inventory (continued)

1. _____

2. _____

3. _____

4. _____

5. _____

6. _____

7. _____

8. _____

9. _____

10. _____

11. _____

12. _____

13. _____

14. _____

15. _____

38. Quickly sizing up a person or situation accurately
39. Having insight
40. Ability to visualize third dimension
41. Acting on gut reactions
42. Other:

## VII. USING ANALYTICAL THINKING OR LOGIC

43. Researching, information-gathering
44. Analyzing, dissection
45. Organizing, classifying
46. Problem-solving
47. Separating important from unimportant
48. Diagnosing
49. Systematizing, putting things in order
50. Comparing, perceiving similarities

_____

_____

_____

_____

_____

_____

_____

_____

_____

_____

_____

_____

_____

_____

*Job Skills Inventory* (continued)

1. _____
2. _____
3. _____
4. _____
5. _____
6. _____
7. _____
8. _____
9. _____
10. _____
11. _____
12. _____
13. _____
14. _____
15. _____

51. Testing,
    screening
52. Reviewing,
    evaluating
53. Other:

VIII. *USING ORIGINALITY
      OR CREATIVITY*
54. Imaginative,
    imagining
55. Inventing,
    creating
56. Designing,
    developing

_____

_____

_____

_____

_____

_____

_____

_____

_____

_____

_____

_____

_____

57. Improvising, experimenting
58. Adapting, improving
59. Other:

IX. *USING HELPFULNESS*

60. Helping, being of service
61. Showing sensitivity to others' feelings
62. Listening
63. Developing rapport
64. Conveying warmth, caring
65. Understanding
66. Drawing people out

*Job Skills Inventory* (continued)

| | 1. | 2. | 3. | 4. | 5. | 6. | 7. | 8. | 9. | 10. | 11. | 12. | 13. | 14. | 15. |
|---|---|---|---|---|---|---|---|---|---|---|---|---|---|---|---|
| | | | | | | | | | | | | | | | |

67. Offering support
68. Demonstrating empathy
69. Representing others' wishes accurately
70. Motivating
71. Sharing credit, appreciation
72. Raising others' self-esteem
73. Healing, curing
74. Counseling, guiding

75. Other:

## X. USING ARTISTIC ABILITIES

76. Composing music

77. Playing musical instrument(s), singing

78. Fashioning or shaping things, materials

79. Dealing creatively with symbols or images

80. Dealing creatively with spaces, shapes, or faces

## Job Skills Inventory (continued)

1.

2.

3.

4.

5.

6.

7.

8.

9.

10.

11.

12.

13.

14.

15.

81. Dealing creatively with colors

82. Conveying feelings and thoughts through body, face, and/or voice tone

83. Conveying feelings and thoughts through drawing, painting

84. Using words on
    a very high
    articulate
    level
85. Other:

XI. *USING LEADERSHIP
    (BEING UP FRONT)*
86. Beginning new
    tasks, ideas,
    projects
87. Taking the
    first move in
    relationships
88. Organizing
89. Leading, direct-
    ing others
90. Promoting change
91. Making decisions
92. Taking risks
93. Getting up
    before a group,
    performing

183

*Job Skills Inventory (continued)*

| | 1. | 2. | 3. | 4. | 5. | 6. | 7. | 8. | 9. | 10. | 11. | 12. | 13. | 14. | 15. |
|---|---|---|---|---|---|---|---|---|---|---|---|---|---|---|---|

94. Selling, promoting, negotiating, persuading

95. Other:

XII. *USING FOLLOW-THROUGH*

96. Using what others have developed

97. Following through on plans, instructions

_____

_____

_____

_____

_____

_____

_____

_____

_____

_____

_____

_____

_____

_____

98. Attending to
    details
99. Classifying,
    recording,
    filing,
    retrieving
100. Other:

2. *Where, or in the service of what, would I like to use my skills? What is important to me? To what purpose am I willing to work eight or more hours per day?*

To illustrate why these questions are important, suppose one of your most enjoyable activities was welding. This would require such skills as "using hands," "using body," "using senses; eyes," and so on. The question is now where do you want to use those skills? You might weld a wagon wheel together. You might use your welding to put together the casing for a nuclear bomb. You could be very happy in one job and not the other.

What makes the difference?

Each is an entirely different job with different value systems, different products, different rewards. So it is not enough simply to know what skills you have. You must also decide where you want to use them.

The "where" questions divide into two broad parts:

a. *Mission or goals:* In the service of what purposes, what issues, what needs, what values, would I like to use the skills I identified? What are my highest goals and values of life?

b. *Effectiveness:* In terms of geography (urban, rural, large or small organization), type of organization, working conditions, where would I most like to use my skills?

Somebody will simply read these questions and immediately come up with answers. If you have always *liked gardening,* for example, then you can consider horticulture, greenhouses, ecology, forestry, or many other related fields.

### PEOPLE ENVIRONMENT

All jobs are ultimately a matter of using your favorite skills with certain kinds of people. The following exercise will help you pinpoint your preferred people environment.

Using the diagram, decide what kind of people you must like to work with:

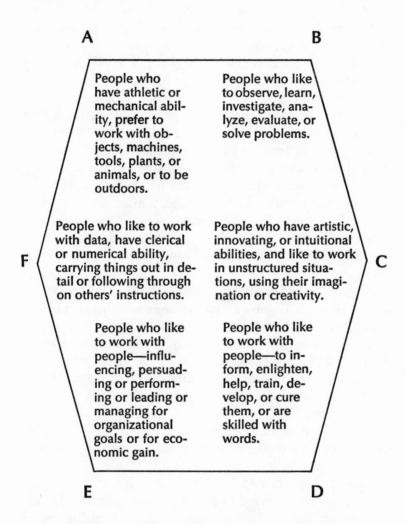

A

B

People who have athletic or mechanical ability, prefer to work with objects, machines, tools, plants, or animals, or to be outdoors.

People who like to observe, learn, investigate, analyze, evaluate, or solve problems.

F

People who like to work with data, have clerical or numerical ability, carrying things out in detail or following through on others' instructions.

People who have artistic, innovating, or intuitional abilities, and like to work in unstructured situations, using their imagination or creativity.

C

People who like to work with people—influencing, persuading or performing or leading or managing for organizational goals or for economic gain.

People who like to work with people—to inform, enlighten, help, train, develop, or cure them, or are skilled with words.

E

D

In your community, find some examples of people who are actually doing the kind of job you listed as being interesting to you. Go talk with them. Ask them:

How did you get into this work?

What do you like most about it?

What do you like least about it?

Where else, in what other kinds of jobs, are people making their living like you do?

3. *In what locations would I be able to do my most effective work? How do I get hired there?*

What you decide you want to do is one thing, but where your job will be located is obviously an important factor. If you are very interested in publishing, for instance, you'll probably have to go to a medium-sized or large city to find work. But what if you don't want to live in a large city? You have a basic conflict that has to be resolved. Or, consider the service situations. John wanted to be a forest ranger but found that the periods of loneliness were distracting him far more than he had imagined. John had to concede that a job around people would be more to his liking.

Your work environment can be almost as important as the work itself. If you're a nature-lover who hates concrete cities, that must be taken into consideration when you're thinking about what kind of work to do. And vice versa. Jobhunting with specifics in mind can often be easier than if you're open to anything. Granted, getting a specific job is not always easy, but at least you know:

a. Where to look, and

b. Why you're looking there.

After that, it's a matter of perseverance, determination, and —sometimes—luck.

After you've located what you think you want to do, you have to go about trying to find a job doing that. Jobhunting can be hard, depressing, and sometimes frightening if you're not certain of what you're looking for. Even when you do know, you can still get turned down, and being turned down is never an easy thing to take.

But jobhunting can also be very rewarding. In some cases, you'll have long interviews; in others, you'll have tests to take or suggestions to make.

For those tired of just looking at ads and filling out applications, there is the nontraditional approach, which works much better in finding a job but takes more effort on your part. This approach involves your taking each of the following steps:

1. Know your skills and talents.

2. Decide what kind of environment you want to work in.

3. Identify a person who has "power" or "knowledge" at the place you want to work and set an appointment to meet with him or her. Your reason for the meeting should be to find out more about this type of work, whether it is what you want, and to get ideas on how to pursue a job in this field.

4. During your interview (keep it to fifteen to twenty minutes), ask questions to find out as much as you can about their work, problems, and background.

5. Thank the person for his/her time and help. Then take your notes home with you and decide whether you would like this kind of work and if this is the place where you would enjoy working. Send a thank-you note in any event.

6. If you decide this is one of the best places for you, prepare a specific written proposal or letter to present to the company on "how my skills and talents can benefit you or your company."

7. Meet again with the same person and share your proposal.

The major difference between this way of finding a job and the more traditional way is your attitude. You are being responsible to your own desires and hope. It's not a question of whether the company wants you, it's whether you feel you can be happy working for them and if you feel your skills will fill a need. Employers may be quite impressed with your sense of purpose and direction.

Where will you go after high school? Into higher education, work, or drifting? The choice is yours. You have to decide. But it's good to keep in mind that it's your life to waste, or live.

# EUGENE NIDA

Dr. Nida writes on the subject of You and Your Concept of the Universe with great depth and understanding. He has traveled to more than seventy-five countries and speaks four different languages and reads in four others. His travels around the world have given him a unique understanding and sensitivity to many different philosophies and cultures.

Dr. Nida has written many books on the subjects of religion and philosophy. He is the Executive Secretary for Translation of the American Bible Society. He received his doctoral degree from the University of Michigan and now lives in Greenwich, Connecticut.

Dr. Nida's keen understanding of the problems of countries throughout the world makes him a man who can offer sound suggestions on how to develop a more realistic concept of the universe.

# *You and Your Concept of the Universe*

The night was pitch-black when we pulled into a roadside diner. This was a midwestern city, and a tough part of town. There at the counter sat two policemen, calmly drinking coffee, munching doughnuts as though nothing could possibly go wrong. After chatting a minute, I said, "Looks like you're not expecting trouble tonight."

I've been thinking ever since about their answer: "'Course not. It's new moon. Give us two weeks to full moon and we'll have plenty of action. Always like that at full moon. Does things to people."

Ancient Rome had much the same idea. They insisted that being out under full moon could cause people to do all kinds of weird things. They called this strange phenomenon "moonstruck." And from them we inherit the word *lunatic*, from the Latin *luna*, meaning "moon."

If you can accept the possibility that human behavior is affected by the moon, how about going one step beyond. . . .

The Brown family moved from St. Petersburg, Florida, to La Jolla, California, because their father was transferred. Richard, their black cat, was everybody's favorite, including the neighbors. So, not wanting to disturb Richard's life, they decided to leave him with the neighbors.

A few weeks after his family moved, Richard disappeared. Two and one-half years later he showed up in the Browns' backyard in La Jolla.

Thousands of miles, by foot, by boat, by truck. How? There he was, the same Richard.

Some people say, "There is kinship with all life." Meaning? Animals and humans have some mysterous relationship, unknown to most people.

What do you think?

You may not think you are influenced by the world around you, but you most certainly are—and even more, you may be influenced by your ideas about the universe.

To understand how our ideas about the universe influence our lives, we need to see how other people view the universe. In a sense, there are almost as many different ideas about the universe as there are people in the world. Yet most of the really important differences can be understood if we group them four ways:

1. Circle versus arrow
2. Junkyard versus machine shop
3. Three yardsticks
4. Closed versus open truth

## Circle Versus Arrow

The most widely held view of our universe can be described as circular. This view is based on the cycle of nature: spring, summer, fall, winter.

With this cycle are the revolving planets and the constellations as well as an endless sequence of plant life: from tiny seeds, tender sprouts, energy-storing leaves, unfolding flowers, back to tiny seeds, ready to begin growth again the following year.

Human life often seems to be part of the same cycle: birth, infancy, childhood, adolescence, adulthood, old age, death. These cycles of nature have sometimes been symbolized as "the wheel of existence" or "the wheel of destiny." For most people who hold this wheel view of the universe, there is really no ultimate progress. Over and over the wheel turns and what may seem like progress is only a delusion.

Liberation from this wheel of existence is usually thought of as an "escape." The Hindu by rituals of purification or the Buddhist by enlightenment, self-discipline, meditation, seeks to remain unperturbed in the midst of life's crises and calamities.

Most so-called tribal people have not thought of the world in terms of a wheel; their view of life might be described as "the way of the beaten path leading nowhere." Theirs is largely a static way. Many of their sons carry on as their fathers and grandfathers did. Many of their daughters imitate the ways of their mothers and grandmothers. Thus the young live only the kind of life the tribe has known generation after generation.

For many persons, the circle view of life suggests identity with nature. They somehow feel related to snowclad mountains, towering pines, soaring eagles, nectar-sipping bees. This view of life has been shown with great appeal in the Buddhist paintings of idyllic mountains which never quite touch the ground, quiet streams inviting meditation, human figures lost in the grandeur of it all.

For some people the world of nature also suggests an unselfish concern for the welfare of others. For whether in bees or baboons, they note that some individuals readily sacrifice themselves for the good of the hive or the band. They are also impressed with how the mother partridge pretends a broken wing and, at the risk of her own life, tries to draw a fox away from the nest of helpless young.

But nature is also cruel. A rabbit nibbles the grass, only to be caught by a hawk, which is soon shot by man. Then the man may die because of malaria parasites introduced into his blood by mosquitoes. And the mosquito? He is caught in full flight by a bat using its sonar sounds to locate prey in the darkest night. Little wonder this circle view of the world so often leads people to pessimism and despair. What chance can one poor human have in such a bloody world?

"We live on the ocean and I wish you could tell me how they know it will be high tide at 4:17 three months from now. How can they predict low tides three months ahead too and never miss one minute? I think that is really fantastic, don't you?"

*—Robin*

In contrast with the circle view of the universe and nature, there is the "arrow" view of the world. The arrow suggests that life is going someplace—at least it is not merely revolving on itself. Of course, the arrow could be pointing in either direction.

For some, the arrow points back to a so-called golden age. These backward-lookers paint the past in glowing colors, even if these colors are only imagined. There are others who want to turn the clock back to something which they believe was better. Often they retreat because they are fearful of the future and the unknown. For them, a tranquil past appeals much more than facing a stormy future.

To most people, however, the arrow symbol suggests progress into the future. For Communists, the ideal is a classless society, which in actual practice moves further and further into the future. For Christians, the ideal of ultimate progress is expressed in the theme of the Kingdom of God on earth. But regardless of the target, the arrow view of the universe means action. It means change rather than contemplative acceptance. The arrow view also means a restless world, constant tension. This is true because change always forces adjustments and adjustments do not come easily. Progress also implies pride in improvements, followed almost immediately by a desire to make things even better.

The possibility of progress, which is a relatively new idea, is aptly expressed in the slogan "The sky's the limit." No limit to progress. No limit to the benefits people can enjoy from work and ingenuity. Anthropologists often speak of such a view of the world as involving the concept of "unlimited good."

> What difference would it make if you believed "there is no ceiling to the possibilities?"
> What difference would it make to mankind?
> What difference would it make to you?

The concept of "unlimited good" is in startling contrast to the way in which most tribal peoples look upon the future and its possibilities. For them the universe contains only so much "soul stuff" (meaning supernatural force which makes possible accumulation of riches or increase of power). Accordingly, if one person is conspicuously richer or more powerful than others, he must have obtained such advantages at the expense of others.

In the society that believes that "soul stuff" is limited, suspicion and jealousy will be the rule. It also follows naturally that the exceptional person here is often cut down to size by force, by sorcery. But in the world of "unlimited good" there is presumably no limit to what a person can acquire, provided he is willing to pay the price in astute planning and hard work.

When people view the world as capable of offering unlimited rewards for effort, they are not so likely to begrudge the riches and power of others. The question is "How can I get my fair share?" Under such circumstances, people are willing to make long-term plans which will pay off even greater rewards.

The arrow view of the universe can also lead to altruism, since people are willing to sacrifice themselves for the sake of a future goal. Sometimes this goal is not only for them but something their children may enjoy. So, freedom and justice in a new and better world challenge some of man's highest endeavors as well as generate the greatest sacrifices.

One must not imagine, however, that a nation inevitably continues with the same view of the world throughout its history. It isn't true either that a person with an arrow view never changes his concepts of the universe.

When people lose confidence in their leaders and feel powerless to improve circumstances, the arrow view becomes a treadmill view. Now there is motion and movement but no one is getting anywhere. Goals become faint, receding even faster than a mirage. So the people declare, "Stop the merry-go-round, I want to get off." What was at one time the exciting hustle and bustle of progress becomes boring, exhausting. As an ancient prophet states it: "Where there is no vision, the people perish."

## Junkyard Versus Machine Shop

On the outskirts of many big cities and even many smaller ones, you can see those piles of rusting junk. Parts of cars, pieces of trucks, leftovers from boilers, steam engines, electric motors all heaped up, scattered around. There they pile high—the victims of accident, chance throwaways.

But over here, in bold contrast, you can see the machine shop with its tall cranes, powerful lifts, massive planers, huge lathes—all functioning so effectively that the end result is something useful, meaningful. Everything makes sense here. Each machine fits together. The various stages of work make sense. Organization at its best.

Different views of the world can be almost as diverse as junkyard and machine shop. Is the universe a result of accident? Is this the result of some "Big Bang" fourteen billion years ago?

Are we (our world, ourselves) only fragments still rushing through space at thousands of miles a second? Are we mere small happenings of matter, time, and space? If so, can the whole thing blow up again any time? What if our earth could be smashed to pieces by some huge meteorite (as in science fiction)? Will our world one day be scorched by atomic bombs dropped at the command of a frightened, power-mad man? Will some groups go crazy and end life for everyone?

> If you knew the sun was crashing toward the earth, what would your first thoughts be?
>
> If it were moving at such a pace that you had a week before it happened, what would you do?

If yours is a junkyard concept of the universe, you might very well conclude that the best thing is to wring every drop of pleasure out of every minute. Why make long-term plans when tomorrow may be the end?

Accordingly, the pleasure principle gains top priority. And if mere personal pleasure finally loses its attraction (after a while it almost always does), you can always take consolation in being a bored, tough-skinned cynic, mocking the loss of nerve in other people.

The whole history of scientific investigation of the universe, however, reveals something quite different from a junkyard. This is true because everywhere we look we discover structure, order, pieces fitting together in incredibly complex and beautiful ways.

Can this universe have begun with some massive explosion? Or did it begin with a quiet evolution? No matter which you choose, on every hand now, behold clear evidence of structure and design.

The planets surrounding our sun (itself just one of two hundred billion stars in the galaxy called Milky Way) reveal amazing structure. Despite their differences in size and distance from the sun, they all revolve around the sun. And they revolve in a broad ellipse with a precision that can be reduced to a neat mathematical formula.

The time a particular planet takes for one orbit of the sun (its year) increases in exact proportion with the average distance of the planet from the sun. How far away are these planets? Some are so far that it would take an astronaut thirty years to traverse our solar system. Yet the movements of these planets together within the solar system can be predicted with split-second accuracy.

For an astronaut to travel to the closest star would require at least 100,000 years. To cross the Milky Way would require more than twenty-five billion years. And how about this? Our galaxy is only one of more than ten billion galaxies! Despite such mind-boggling distances, the relation between heavenly bodies resembles the machine shop far more than the junkyard chaos.

If, instead of looking at the vast universe of starry space, we look into the minute realm of the atom, we see equally elaborate structures. Nuclei consisting of neutons and protons, circled by fast-moving electrons, remind us of miniature solar systems. The position any chemical element occupies in the order of elements is based on the number of its electrons. One for hydrogen, two for helium, three for lithium, four for beryllium, on and on for more than ninety basic elements.

Even in the intensely hot interiors of the stars, processes are at work building up atoms into more and more complex structures. In this sense physical matter itself may be said to evolve. But protons, electrons, and neutrons are by no means the only particles of force discovered in the nuclei of atoms. These nuclei contain systems within systems, so complex that ultimate forces or entities may never be discovered.

One need not look, however, either to the vastness of the sky or to the smallness of the atom for structure. For example, even though no two snowflakes are ever exactly alike, they are all subject to the same structural law. Know the law? It is the law requiring all basic angles of the crystals to be sixty degrees!

Human behavior also reveals structure, perhaps best illustrated by language. Sentences are not merely collections of words thrown together in any order. Words are built into phrases, phrases into clauses, clauses into full sentences. In the English language, adjectives go with nouns, adverbs with verbs, and prepositional phrases can go with both. Most speakers of a language are quite unaware of structure. Children acquire amazing competence with words long before they study grammar. Unconsciously they grasp the rules which make communication possible.

Similarly, the ways in which we use first names, nicknames, full names, and titles are structured in amazingly complex ways. For example, among classmates or teammates first names are normally used, but if people are good friends and if a touch of humor is allowed, nicknames are appropriate. Teachers, bosses, the unfamiliar are usually addressed by title and last name (except behind their backs, when other nicknames are employed). Well-known persons, especially those famous in their own line (actors, scholars), are often referred to by their last names. Athletes may more often be mentioned by nicknames.

Once these so-called rules are described we readily recognize the system. Yet we may have unconsciously been applying the rules for years without giving it even a thought. Similar structured behavior can be discovered in the way people carry on conversations, the way they shop at supermarkets, the way they react to illness, bad news, good news.

Since the world around us is so amazing, and since even our everyday lives seem loaded with mystery, some people have concluded that earthly life must not be the end of existence. "Anything as wonderful as this has to carry on!" they reason. Accordingly, man comes up with many different beliefs about life beyond death. For some of these, death is regarded as a kind of birth. And this belief is frequently symbolized by burying a corpse in the position of an unborn child, ready to be reborn into the next life.

Though the universe may be thought of as resembling either the disorder of a junkyard or the structure of a machine shop, most people's actual view of their world is a rather untidy combination of both ideas. The Mongbandi people of Zaire recognize the basic goodness of the universe. They attribute this to their god Chuchu. Chuchu created the world and gave people many fine gifts. But they believe that because people were noisy and quarrelsome and because their fires kept driving smoke into Chuchu's eyes, he could not put up with them any longer and so went away, leaving them to the mercy of mischievous evil spirits.

In Europe and America, the deists (believers in God) of the eighteenth century had a more sophisticated explanation than that of the Mongbandi. Yet it amounted to much the same concept of the universe. They insisted that God, like a master watchmaker, created the world. Then having once set it going, he let it be governed by its own laws, subject to its own imperfections.

The ancient Persians interpreted the experience of both good and evil in the universe as the result of competition between two gods: one good, one bad. As ways of trying to reconcile the contradictions in the universe, other peoples have held beliefs about gods and demons, good and evil spirits, God and the devil.

> "Last year there was this boy from India in our class. He was an exchange student. He believes in reincarnation and he is very sure that he has lived before and will come back in a different form or as another person. His beliefs are very old. When our class discussed this, we wondered if in the future our beliefs will be a combination of what we believe now, plus old things, and new things. Do you suppose so?"
>
> *—Andy*

## Three Yardsticks

Remember how, when you were growing up, every so often you would stand straight beside a yardstick? It made you feel good to gain a half inch, three-quarters of an inch, one inch. I can remember the day I passed five feet.

Different cultures also set up yardsticks of accomplishment in order to measure whether their deeds are right or wrong, whether they are reaching their full potential. Or are they only fumbling along? Problem: Find the right yardstick. This is absolutely essential because to measure anything, there must be some basis for comparison, a standard. To find such yardsticks, people have generally looked to what they believe has made them what they are.

The most obvious yardstick with which many people measure themselves is nature itself. People often look to animal nature, for in an important sense, man is an animal.

Both human and animal bodies contain essentially the same building blocks, called amino acids. These are intricate double spirals of the chromosomes in the nucleus of each cell of animal bodies.

The human body is also organized much like that of the animals: head, limbs, trunk, digestive organs. And all similarly placed. Moreover, humans reproduce much like monkeys and apes. Recently psychologists have even taught chimpanzees to communicate with men on a simple level. By means of plastic symbols as substitutes for what are words in human speech, these animals can communicate with their trainers and vice versa.

It is little wonder many persons have concluded that man is essentially an animal and only differs quantitatively from other animals. He may seem to be more intelligent than animals, but is he? (Did you ever hear about the man who said, "The more I see of my neighbors, the more I think of my dog"?) In a sense, people are more clever with their hands than animals. They are not as locked into their environment as animals. And in civilizations like ours, man has altered his environment with clothing, buildings, fire, air conditioners.

Yet, despite these seeming advantages, some concluded that man is just a better animal. True, he is more efficient, but not basically different from other animals. So, they contend, not being "different from" animals, but being only "more of" an animal, man must be judged by a yardstick applicable to animals. For many persons such a view of man includes looking at man's family structures—sex life, squabbling, morals. "See," they say, "man is little more than a high-class animal." In other words, expect more of people than animals, but not much more!

Most people, however, believe this animal yardstick for man is inadequate. They insist man can't be measured by the same standards as animals. Furthermore, they contend that his distinctive qualities are the only valid ones by which he can and should be judged. One such distinction is man's imagination. By his imagination he can make plans for the future and carry them out.

Instead of only adjusting to circumstances, man can change circumstances with his language. Although the vocabulary of most English-speaking persons may not consist of more than thirty thousand words, they can talk about millions of things. They can describe countless events. In addition, each speaker has an inquisitive nature which leads him to explore his environment and even himself. So he finds not just something to eat, but he learns, he understands.

Whether man is solving riddles of an X-ray emanating from powerful objects in outer space or watching a hummingbird hover over a tiny flower, he comprehends. Man also has a drive to beautify his surroundings for apparently no practical purpose. The decorated cake may not taste better. Neither does an intricately carved paddle made by a Palauan native in the South Pacific help to steer an outrigger any faster. But they do add meaning. So by countless means, men and women have built-in value systems, which make them quite different from both animals and computers.

The human brain may be likened to a computer and the mind to a computer program, but each person also has what is often called "the heart," "soul," "the inner being" —by any name it gives us a system for attaching value. To people, to things, to happenings we add meaning. And from these values, these meanings, we construct our system of ethics and our elaborate rules for justice.

If we accept the fact that man possesses these distinctive qualities, we have a basis for judging how satisfactory our world is. Now we can help people measure up to their potential. Now in a real sense we can say "Man is the measure of all things." Yet to this conclusion many people have strong objections. They say, "You are judging mankind by mankind, which is like comparing a yardstick to a yardstick." Accordingly, many of the world's most profound thinkers have insisted that humankind must be measured against something greater, better than itself.

Always, in every society, there are those who insist man needs something transcendental (something which is beyond man). Because of this, in one way or another, all cultures have reached out for something supernatural. Often these supernatural beings are made in the people's own image; that is, supernatural beings which resemble the people themselves. These would be like the gods and goddesses of the Greeks and Romans. Like people, they loved and lied, helped and hated, made war and made peace.

In Judaism and Christianity, mankind is believed to be made in the image of God, and therefore the only proper yardstick for man would be those standards which God Himself has set. For the Christian, the best-known yardstick is to be found in the Sermon on the Mount. For the Buddhist, the standard is a supernatural enlightenment which breaks through the darkness of human delusion and opens the way for the ultimate experience of Nirvana.

This reaching for the supernatural or being reached by the supernatural is the keystone of all religion. In this sense, religion is distinct from philosophy. Though a philosopher may construct a system of belief which involves God, a devotee of a religion insists on communicating with God. He receives messages in the form of prophecies, dreams, visions. He sends messages through prayer, offerings, sacrifices. In this way, supernatural beings and powers come to the aid of people for rescuing them from danger, healing their bodies, giving them moral courage, protecting them from evil.

This third yardstick is the way in which people measure up to standards set by their God. The ultimate seems to have been formulated by Christ for Christians: "Be perfect even as your heavenly Father is perfect."

> Letter from a friend:
> "I get so sick and tired of people telling me how I ought to behave. Why can't I just make my own rules?"
>
> How would you answer this friend?

## Closed Versus Open Truth

Both your concepts about the universe and your attitude toward those very concepts have a powerful influence on what you are. They make a big difference in how you live. They determine what pleasure you find in life.

No doubt you have met people who are absolutely sure that what they believe is the only way. We all tend to be somewhat like that, for in many respects it is so much easier to believe than to think. To think honestly is often disturbing and, because this is true, some people want their leaders to think for them.

Though we all admire a person who has strong convictions, we must beware of leaders who insist that they always know what is good for us. Those who feel they have a monopoly on truth can be terribly dangerous. A German wallpaper-hanger named Hitler proved that for certain. Others have, too. Yet the tragedy is that some people want leaders who give the impression "I'm always right. I have an exclusive on truth." So the saying goes, "There is no fool such a big fool that he cannot get other fools to follow him, if only he can hide his doubts."

Closed truth tends always to force everyone into a common mold. Think the same thoughts, mimic the same slogans, applaud the secret police as they jail the "queer people." An excellent example of the society is the beehive. Absolute efficiency and every bee perfectly programmed to do its work.

On the human level we have another example in the Quechua Indian society. Before the arrival of Pizarro in Peru, every person, every village, every region was dependent upon the one central authority, the Inca. Not surprising therefore that Pizarro, with only 62 horsemen and 106 footsoldiers, was able to overthrow an empire of more than five million people. Once the Inca had been destroyed, the beehive structure collapsed, even as a hive will die when the queen bee is killed.

Immense strides in scientific discovery and greater knowledge concerning the universe can lead to a false conclusion that truth is constantly becoming more closed, and because it is, we can afford to be more dogmatic. Such an attitude does not, however, stem from science. It comes from scientism as popularized in science fiction. Scientism, by drawing dogmatic conclusions from scientific theories, is frighteningly dangerous. And it is especially dangerous when it justifies one race concluding that it is a superior race destined to force its ideas on other nations.

Humility is always one requirement of true science. And true science always recognizes the uncertainty of its conclusions. Scientific descriptions of the universe can never be absolute and conclusions must never become dogmas.

Yet you are wise to come to some conclusions and make them the basis of your personal belief. If you do you will find that your concepts about the physical universe can make a tremendous difference in the way you live, the values you hold, the friends you make.

Some people say the most important concept of all is your belief in God. Do you think of God as an impersonal being out there in space or as "the man upstairs"? To you, is he like a celestial Santa Claus, or is He a personal God, creator not only of the starry heavens but also of you? You can see how the answer to those questions could make a big difference to people, not only in this life but also as they look beyond this life.

No one can know for sure that the next life will be like. The Apostle Paul said the difference would be like the contrast between seeds planted in the ground and the beautiful plants which emerge later from the soil. All the religions of the world have in one way or another sensed that life here is not the end.

The message of eternal life has brought hope and courage to millions. That would be something, wouldn't it, if the God who has made history possible has also prepared for you something even far more meaningful than you have ever dreamed?

Yet, no matter what eternal life may be like, you can see what it would add to our lives if we could say for sure: "God's universe is no junkyard and I am not going to be tossed onto some rubbish heap of history. My destiny is a full, rich life, now, and I will live it in the light of life's eternal meaning, too."

"What is your concept of the universe?"

"That question," said the speaker, "is more important than any other you will ever answer."

Now, why?

"Because," the man continued, "it is the law of life that you gather to yourself according to the major focus of your mind. Like attracts like. Positive thoughts bring positive returns. The negative draws negative."

# Author's Note

This book is part of a program called Quest. Quest was established in 1975. It is a nonprofit organization developing programs for public and private high schools, and other youth-serving organizations. Through the support of the W. K. Kellogg Foundation, the George Gund Foundation, and the *Reader's Digest*, Quest has developed a course for teenagers and their parents. The course deals with the personal concerns which are described in this book. The students will learn about life and how to be better prepared to face it, whether in a high school, a college dorm, on the job, or at a party with friends.

The course is designed to teach basic skills for effective living through active involvement in the community, along with an opportunity to attend a six-day intern program with other students. This intern program is designed to give the students opportunities to learn how their talents can be used to build deeper friendships, better understand themselves, and provide volunteer service to help others when they return to their community. Also, the parents have an opportunity to be involved in a similar program designed to provide a link between teenagers and parents.

If you are interested in receiving further information about teacher training, instructional materials, and how this program might be implemented into your local school district or a youth organization in your area, additional information can be obtained by contacting:

QUEST INCORPORATED
2707 North Main Street
Findlay, Ohio 45840
(419) 424-9693